destinations

a Compass for K–12 Music Educators

G-7689

destinations
a Compass for K–12 Music Educators

Joseph Alsobrook

edited by Michael D. Worthy, PhD

GIA Publications, Inc.
Chicago

For Micah and Jordan,

two enthusiastic talents who lost to music education

Destinations

A Compass for K–12 Music Educators

Joseph Alsobrook

Edited by Michael D. Worthy, PhD
Art design / layout: Martha Chlipala

G-7689
ISBN: 978-1-57999-774-8

contents

acknowledgments

This is a book of mental sweat and sacrifice. I have done the sweating and three very special people have done the giving. Thank you Connie, Micah, and Jordan..for your patience, your presence, and for enduring arthur weather. Your songs are a blessing of inexpressible measure.

This is also a work of wisdom from educational and musical spheres—a seemingly logical mix for exploring music education. To all the artists, educators, and leaders whose brilliance graces these pages, thank you. For both pre-service and in-service music educators, you have fashioned a book that not only enlightens, but also sings!

Despite my best efforts to speak intelligibly, this text would be akin to gibberish without the help of a great teacher. "A hundred thousand thank you's," Mom, for sharing your way of words.

Every author needs an anchor. Thank you, Mike—musician and scholar extraordinaire—for your scrutiny, refinement, and impeccable ability to see what needs to be seen. I am most grateful.

Opinion and perspective are two very different points of view. Thank you to Lindenwood University for giving me the opportunity to learn from so many exemplary educators, both on and off campus. Without these experiences, this puzzle would forever remain as pieces.

Last, but light years from least, thank you to all of the learners who have crossed my path. Through your amazing accomplishments, resilience, and even failures, you have taught me the real definition of "teacher." What a tremendous honor and privilege it's been to be your student!

THANK YOU CLARITY,

THANK YOU, THANK YOU SILENCE

ALANIS MORISSETTE • "THANK U"
SONGWRITERS: ALANIS MORISSETTE, GLEN BALLARD

prelude

True or False?

When you're knee-deep in alligators it's hard to remember
that your initial objective was to drain the swamp.

—Unknown

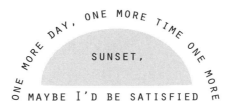

ONE MORE DAY, ONE MORE TIME ONE MORE

SUNSET,

MAYBE I'D BE SATISFIED

BUT THEN AGAIN, I KNOW WHAT IT WOULD DO,

LEAVE ME WISHING STILL FOR ONE MORE DAY WITH YOU

DIAMOND RIO • "ONE MORE DAY WITH YOU"
SONGWRITERS: STEVEN DALE JONES, BOBBY TOMBERLIN

2

For decades, songwriters have danced with the digit known as "one." Perhaps this is for good reason. When you think about it, one is a highly influential number. It takes just one sarcastic comment to hurt our feelings, one mysterious hair to squelch an appetite, and one over-ambitious bari sax player to ruin a perfectly superior performance. On the other hand, it takes just one smile to brighten someone's day, one change of heart to mend a broken relationship, and one ounce of attention to alter the course of a child's life.

The solitary symbol is also applicable to those who walk the path of music education. In fact, music educators are *one* in many, many ways. Brace yourself. This could get ugly.

MAKE OF OUR LIVES ONE LIFE

DAY AFTER DAY, ONE LIFE

NOW IT BEGINS, NOW WE START

ONE HAND, ONE HEART

"ONE HAND, ONE HEART" • FROM WEST SIDE STORY
SONGWRITERS: LEONARD BERNSTEIN, STEPHEN SONDHEIM

For starters, music educators share students who are growing up in an increasingly complex society. Endless options, fast paces, instant gratification, and dazzling displays of technology epitomize the world in which our students live. With very little effort, students can get what they want, when they want, and in a vast array of colors, shapes, and sizes. Adventure in infinite form lies at the very tips of their fingers; the world, for all practical purposes, is just a click away. Thus, chips and bytes have gnawed the adventure of investigation to shreds. Research that once took hours can be done in minutes, calculations that once took minutes can be done in nanoseconds, and information that should probably never be discovered appears in a flash. Web-based educator, author, and instructional designer, Tom March (2006), warns of the hazards inherent to the "Whatever, Whenever, Wherever":

> Unlimited, ubiquitous personalized media gratification is unlike anything we've ever had to contend with, and just letting it happen isn't a good idea. Envision the horror and glory of getting whatever we want, whenever and wherever we want it. Online gambling, panda cams, cam girls, hate groups, online fantasy role-playing games, the Worldwide Association of Seaweed Processors—it's all there. All we have to do is choose. (p. 16)

Is there any wonder why many students quickly become dissatisfied and frustrated with things that take time, like school? Is there any wonder why keeping students engaged and on task is far from a simple proposition? Too much of too many "good things" and perspectives become skewed while patience runs short. And it's never enough. Students not only learn to expect more, but they become truly convinced that they are entitled to more.

> As an enemy of happiness, entitlement is a subjective and emotional reaction that justifies and, even defends, dissatisfaction. An entitled perspective places a stamp labeled "Not Enough" over the lenses in which we view life. When we feel that we are not getting what we deserve, it is easy to justify feeling miserable and dissatisfied. Entitlement is able to steal all that is precious in our lives simply by blinding us to the value. Through lenses of "Not Enough," our view of the world becomes restricted, distorted, and self-absorbed. (Billings, 2003, p. 16)

The impact of too much, too soon, and too easily, and surely the reverse—too little, too late, too arduously—may also have ethical repercussions. For example, following a benchmark survey in 1992, the Josephson Institute has conducted a national survey of the ethics of American youth every two years. In 2008, data was gathered through a survey of nearly 30,000 students in high schools across the United States. According to the report:

4

- 93% are satisfied with their personal ethics and character.
- 83% from public and religious private schools confessed they lied to a parent about something significant.
- 64% cheated on a test.
- 36% used the Internet to plagiarize an assignment.
- 30% admitted stealing from a store within the past year.
- 23% stole something from a parent or other relative.
- 20% stole something from a friend.
  (Josephson Institute, 2008 Summary, § 1–4)

To be completely fair, however, we really shouldn't rush to blame progress for all the ills of youth. To resist progress is to resist reality. Childhood is indeed changing, but students do not become inclined to lie, cheat, or steal without being placed at risk by adults. For example, in *The Day America Told the Truth*, 90 percent of the adults surveyed admitted they lie regularly and 7 percent said they would kill a stranger for $10 million (Patterson and Kim, 1991).

Making matters even worse, in a predominantly double-income society with escalating divorce rates and widespread single-parent families, students are subject to many parenting and supervision models. Children still go through the stages that children have always gone through; the difference is that children go through these stages at faster paces and with different types of adult guidance. Multiply the messengers and mixed messages quickly abound. This includes topics like provocative symbolism, profanity, study habits, the virtues of altruism, or even how to wear clothes. Case in point: A middle school teacher frequently begins class by saying, "Boys, stand up and pull up your pants." That's right. Belt work.

Are you starting to see a pattern? "Whether it is because of the media, the lack of parent involvement, the dearth of traditional families, or simply an adult-centered society, teachers often end up with classes filled with too many students with too many problems" (Boers, 2001, p. 51). John Taylor Gatto (1991), New York City's Teacher of the Year in 1989, 1990, and 1991 and New York State Teacher of the Year in 1991, paints an even bleaker picture:

> Rich or poor, schoolchildren cannot concentrate on anything for very long. They have a poor sense of time past and to come; they are mistrustful of intimacy (like the children of divorce they really are); they hate solitude, are cruel, materialistic, dependent, passive, violent, timid in the face of the unexpected, addicted to distraction. (¶ 29)

Perhaps this is why the U.S. Census Bureau (2005) reported that in 2004 only 56 percent of the nation's 18- and 19-year-olds had high school credentials. Perhaps this is why initiative is a flickering commodity and failure is an ever-increasing option in the minds of far too many. Perhaps all of these factors led Steinberg (1996) to claim that students are not becoming less intelligent, but less interested in being educated. Perhaps "reality" is the motivation for school administrators to prepare student handbooks that specifically forbid things like concealed weapons, firearms, chains, live bullets, Chinese stars, clubs, night sticks, num chucks, lasers, stun guns, knives, mace, pepper spray, look-alike weapons, shotguns, knuckles, projectiles, rifles, and switchblades. In the end, who can be surprised by this disheartening countdown that exists among America's youth?

- Every 6 hours a child is killed by abuse or neglect.
- Every 5 hours a child or teen commits suicide.
- Every 4 minutes a child is arrested for a drug offense.
- Every 3 hours a child or teen is killed by a firearm.
- Every 2 days 4,734 high school students drop out.
- Every minute a baby is born to a teen mother.
- Every second a public school student is suspended.
  (Children's Defense Fund, 2008, p. 2)

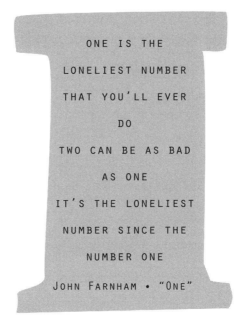

ONE IS THE
LONELIEST NUMBER
THAT YOU'LL EVER
DO
TWO CAN BE AS BAD
AS ONE
IT'S THE LONELIEST
NUMBER SINCE THE
NUMBER ONE
JOHN FARNHAM • "ONE"

Another thing we share in common is a knack for over-extending ourselves. Each year, teachers spend an average of $443 of their own money to meet the needs of their students (National Education Association, 2003, p. 51). Each week, teachers spend an average of fifty hours on instructional duties, including an average of twelve hours each week on non-compensated, school-related activities such as grading papers, bus duty, and club advising (NEA, 2003, pp. 42–43). Music educators, however, like to stretch themselves even thinner. In fact, you would be hard pressed to find a veteran music teacher who is not all too familiar with the following scenario:

6:00 a.m. . . . arrive at school, open building, turn on the lights, and make coffee for the custodians

6:30 a.m. . . . fix copier

6:45 a.m. . . . make copies

7:00 a.m. . . . greet students, hold sectionals

7:55 a.m. . . . search for scores

8:00 a.m. . . . teach first hour

8:55 a.m. . . . teach second hour

9:45 a.m. . . . travel to another school

10:00 a.m. . . . teach a second "second" hour

11:00 a.m. . . .teach third hour

12:00 p.m. . . .gulp down lunch in office while doing paperwork

12:25 p.m. . . .teach fourth hour

1:20 p.m. . . .travel back to home school

1:35 p.m. . . .visit the restroom (finally!)

1:40 p.m. . . .spend planning hour making copies that didn't get done earlier, return phone calls

2:20 p.m. . . .teach last hour

3:15 p.m. . . .report for bus duty (forgot umbrella)

3:30 p.m. . . .attend a meeting (wet from bus duty)

4:30 p.m. . . .give a private lesson

5:00 p.m. . . .give another private lesson

5:30 p.m. . . .hit the drive-thru for dinner

6:00 p.m. . . .greet students as they begin to arrive for the concert

6:30 p.m. . . .change into concert attire in the storage closet

7:00 p.m. . . .initiate warm-up

7:30 p.m. . . .begin concert

9:00 p.m. . . .end concert

9:02 p.m. . . .visit with students and parents

9:25 p.m. . . .change back into real clothes

9:30 p.m. . . .stack chairs, move stands or risers

9:45 p.m. . . .begin turning off lights and locking doors

10:00 p.m. . . .call home before everyone goes to bed

10:15 p.m. . . .lock the front door and head for the car

10:16 p.m. . . .greet two students who are still waiting for rides

10:30 p.m. . . .greet first parent to show up

10:45 p.m. . . .ask remaining student, "Are you sure your mom is on her way?"

10:59 p.m. . . .greet sister who (finally) arrives to pick up her brother

11:04 p.m. . . .stress from thoughts of imperfections at the concert

11:25 p.m. . . .arrive at home

11:57 p.m. . . .set alarm for half past ridiculous

ONE LOVE ONE BLOOD
ONE LIFE
YOU GOT TO DO WHAT YOU SHOULD

U2 • "ONE"
SONGWRITERS: ADAM CLAYTON, DAVE EVANS,
PAUL HEWSON, LARRY MULLEN, JR.

Music educators also share the "character-building" quality of resilience. If the meteorologist says there is a 10 percent chance of snow, we secretly hope for a snow day, but we keep it to ourselves and carry on. We dream of "real food" for lunch, but we survive just fine on yogurt, pretzels, and diet soda. We would love to be showered with praise, but we get by on an occasional "thank you." We need accompanists, but we manage with recordings. We dream of the day people will leave us alone and let us get some work done, but we stop, smile, and listen to anyone who needs us. We want soundproof spaces for our students to practice, but we compromise by using closets and hallways. And just once we would like to have all of the percussion instruments called for in the score, but we get it done with wind chimes from Wal-Mart's garden section and coffee cans filled with beans.

ONE IS BREAKIN' INTO TWO,

AND MY HEART IS TURNIN' BLUE

AND YOU STILL DON'T GET IT, DO YOU…

SO BEFORE THAT DAMAGE IS DONE

LET'S START BACK OVER AT ONE

FAITH HILL • "ONE"
SONGWRITERS:
BEKKA BRAMLETT, BILLY BURNETTE, ANNIE ROBOFF

The hits just keep on coming—yet another bond is challenging contexts in which to teach. Jensen (2005) brings this premise to bright light:

> To the student's brain, biologically relevant school stimuli includes opportunities to make friends (or find mates), quench thirst or hunger, notice a change in the weather, or interact with classroom visitors. All the while, the student's brain is concerned with avoiding the dangers of embarrassment, failure, or harm. These last three are actually what typical students care about most! Yet we ask them to orient their attention on the curriculum topic at hand and to maintain that attention until instructed otherwise, even if this means continuing to listen, read, or work on a single task for up to an hour. They're supposed to do this day in and day out in the midst of a gossip-ridden, physically active, emotionally sensitive, and highly social environment…Add to this mix of attentional challenges the physical environments of the typical classroom—sub-standard lighting, poorly regulated temperatures, constant walk-in distractions, unergonomic "party rental" chair designs—and you're left with "Mission Impossible."
> (pp. 35–36)

In the realm of music education, however, this is just scratching the surface. Veteran teachers would no doubt agree that virtually all positions are accompanied by a host of additional annoyances that steal time and energy. Life coaches call such things "tolerations," and for music teachers, they might include jammed copiers, parents who call once a week and talk for at least thirty minutes, concert attendees who call intermission "half-time," purchase orders, yearbook pictures, students who are incapable of remembering a pencil, neediness (I need a pass, another copy of the music that I lost, a new reed, my horn fixed, less work and more credit for doing so, the report, the invoice, the entry form) and, of course, walking in brass players' spit. Hmmm. Which character from *The Wizard of Oz* is best suited to become a music educator: the lion, the tin man, or the scarecrow?

Each year also brings assured obstacles like first-chair players who quit, switches to block scheduling, leaking roofs in the music library, zero budgets, performance pressure, and uniforms two sizes too small. In response to a question aimed at "major issues of concern," MENC bloggers (2007, November) list a host of frustrations, including scheduling problems, poor facilities, student behavior, teaching schedules that require "twice as much work with three times as many students to be done in half the time," and not enough prep time, funding, support from administration, mentoring and support, time with students, meaningful professional development opportunities, or cohesiveness within K–12 programs—vivid reminders of the all-too-frequent disconnect between reality and a music teacher's expectations.

We're not through yet. Consider the fact that music programs are often appraised by how many students are served. Thus, while the rest of education is fighting for smaller class sizes, music teachers are busy recruiting more and more students. Unfortunately, however, this is another steep hill to climb because music education is an enterprise that is plagued with warped perceptions. But why? Aren't media mockeries of school music funny (e.g., "This one time, at band camp…")? Haven't clear messages about the value of music education been presented through the "Save the Music" campaign? Isn't performing "school music" in an empty auditorium for three judges a significant undertaking?

Considering the external challenges, the internal challenges, and the recurrent strains on positive attributes like resilience and tolerance, it should come as no surprise that burnout, music teacher shortages, the issuing of emergency licenses to those who are far from "highly qualified," and sparse applicants for vacant positions exemplify yet another link among music educators.

RELAX, MAX

YOUR NERVES ARE JUST LIKE JUMPIN' JACKS, MAX

YOUR HEART IS THUMPIN' WITH A CRAZY SOUND

HEAR IT POUND

BUMPIN', BUMPIN', BUMPIN',

JUMPIN' UP AND DOWN

DINAH WASHINGTON • "RELAX, MAX"

So put it all together: the drama, the challenges, the "sad songs" that are inherent to music education. Gasp! Too much? Too soon? Possibly. Yet aren't these things worthy of our attention? Don't these realities that we share matter? Of course they do. Fortunately, however, this is far from where the story ends. Just because something "matters" doesn't mean it has to exhaust us entirely. That would be far from sensible, actually, because things that matter have something very striking in common: they will change. For students, what matters today is being first in line, earning first chair, sitting at the cool lunch table, wearing trendy clothes, and "looking good" in the eyes of their peers. On the weekend, it's sleeping until noon, winning a soccer game, and texting for hours at a time. But they're really no different than the rest of us.

For music teachers, what matters today might be figuring out why the actual funds collected from the fruit sale don't match the invoice, reserving the auditorium for the concert scheduled for next Tuesday, and making copies for third hour. At home, it's dinner, laundry, and recording a favorite television program. On the weekend, it's getting the oil changed, house cleaning, paying bills, and figuring out what in the world to do with first hour on Monday.

In the school community at large, what matters right now may be differentiated instruction, professional learning communities, high-stakes testing, or No Child Left Behind. A few decades ago, it was keeping pregnant teachers and gum out of the classroom; today it's pregnant students and guns.

> Like nineteenth-century medicine men, everybody is promoting everything, whether there is any evidence that it works or not. Over here we have vouchers, charters, privatization, longer school days, summer school, and merit pay. Over there we have the frequent testing of students, the testing of teachers, smaller class size, report cards on schools, and high-stakes accountability. And over here, a very special offer: student uniforms, flag-raising ceremonies every morning, the posting of the Ten Commandments on schoolhouse walls, and sophisticated diagnostic instruments to identify children at risk for acting violently—when many administrators and teachers can't even identify children who need glasses. (Comer, 2001, ¶ 1)

Indeed, education has evolved, is evolving, and will likely continue to evolve. People will come and people will go, new ideas will flow, popular practices will change, and even the most somber statistics will rise and fall, *including the information in this chapter*. There is no way around it. In an enterprise as large and all encompassing as education, things that matter are things in constant flux.

Rich in contrast to this phenomenon, thankfully, lies another dimension to education, a dimension that remains unchanged. It's an interesting paradox: what matters most is in a state of constant change; what means the most remains the same. Soaring high above the tide of things that "matter" is the stable heart of education: an overarching agenda to support the developing child. From coast to coast and border to border, educators have always agreed that students go to school to leave school bigger, stronger, faster, smarter, wiser, and healthier than when they arrived. In essence, education exists to change lives for the better.

> I GUESS IT DON'T MATTER HOW OLD YOU ARE
> OR HOW OLD ONE LIVES TO BE
> I GUESS IT BOILS DOWN TO WHAT WE DID WITH OUR LIVES
> AND HOW WE DEAL WITH OUR OWN DESTINIES
> JOHN MELLENCAMP • "THE REAL LIFE"

For music educators, the means of contributing to this mission is music, which brings us to the heart of this discussion. Do you remember the moment you were captivated by music? At one point or another music stole your heart, captivated your thoughts, and stirred your soul. But this didn't happen all by itself. You had help. Somehow—despite the challenges of the day—the teachers who crossed your path helped you to become something very special. Through their assistance, guidance, example and, no doubt, encouragement, you became a "real" musician…with all the rights and privileges therein. It is now your turn; the opportunity now is to give back.

Before proceeding with this charge, there is an important choice to make. Will you be consumed by challenge and focus almost entirely on survival? Or, as *living proof* that music has immense power to change lives in wondrous and welcome ways, will you accept the challenge and focus on paying forward the gifts that only music can share?

For those who choose the latter, for those whose priority is to equip students for meaningful interaction with the multi-musical experience known as life, you are hereby invited to take a journey—an odyssey of infinite magnitude with no definitive end. The destinations you seek will be as unique as they are united, and when you find that you have more questions than answers, your aims are becoming increasingly clear.

Destination: Expectation points to the overarching goals of music education—the desired results after all is said and done. This is no small detail. Shouldn't a professional music educator be able to describe, in great detail, what an accomplished learner "looks like" after full participation in a K–12 program of study? In contrast, aimlessness knows no bounds. Without clear, guiding intentions, won't any wind suffice?

Even the most meaningful goals are silent without a voice. In defense of such an occurrence, *Destination: Transformation* reflects the metamorphosis that must occur to make fantasy a reality. At its best, the results are clear and measurable pathways to consequential growth and achievement.

Destination: Invitation is synonymous with creativity and motivation. How are we making music education irresistible? How are we responding to the challenge of advancing music education and encouraging the study and making of music by *all?* Are we doing enough? Could we do even more? Does the wisdom of Tom Szews, a professional in the field of telecommunications, have any relevance to music education in the 21st century? "Because we can provide either service, we objectively recommend the solution that best meets a customer's specific needs, not ours" (*Business Wire,* 2006, ¶ 4).

14

Destination: Illumination is brilliance during the "live" moments of teaching—when time either crawls or disappears. The plans have been drawn, the materials are in place, attendance has been taken, and it's just you and your students. This is your chance to actually teach! Only one question really counts: How will you make the most of these few hours?

Destination: Inspiration is equivalent to a concept all teachers must concede: There is always a better way. Finding such a treasure is, of course, no easy task. A good place to begin, however, is reflecting on answers to one wretched question: How do I wax or wane success? Alas, it's one thing to know what you want. It's entirely another to know what you must give up before you get it.

In the end, look carefully…very, very carefully. With any luck you'll find yourself far from running in place, yet right back where you started.

Let the journey begin!

destination: expectation

LIGHT TOMORROW WITH TODAY!

—ELIZABETH BARRETT BROWNING

Considering everything you know about physical, cognitive, and socioemotional development, as well as everything you understand about age-appropriate musical outcomes, take a moment to imagine an accomplished learner after full participation in K–12 music education. Focus your thoughts on learning with lasting value and consequence, or the most important ways in which the students will be different after the experience is complete.

Did you think about the curriculum guide collecting dust in your office? Were your thoughts dominated by performance—polished perfection crowned with the title "one"? Maybe you had thoughts of students practicing daily, meeting deadlines, and stopping when you stop? Or were they just quiet?

Congratulations! You have just experienced the joy of possibility thinking… or perhaps the dark side of such a thought process: when fantasy collides with reality. Either way, there was bound to be a glimpse into the journey of **Expectation**—the quest to clarify the nature of consequential music education, to "see" an accomplished student musician with great clarity, or to establish a clear perspective of why students should show up in the first place.

16

YOU SUDDENLY HEAR A BELL,

AND RIGHT AWAY YOU CAN TELL...

THIS COULD BE THE HEART OF SOMETHING

THIS COULD BE THE START OF SOMETHING BIG!

STEVE LAWRENCE • "THIS COULD BE THE START OF SOMETHING BIG"
SONGWRITER: STEVE ALLEN

I

THAT IS WHAT LEARNING IS.
YOU SUDDENLY
UNDERSTAND SOMETHING
YOU'VE UNDERSTOOD
ALL YOUR LIFE,
BUT IN A
NEW WAY.

—DORIS
LESSING

Despite the extraordinary advances in teaching and learning that have evolved over the years, one of the unfortunate trademarks of education is fiddling with language. This makes talking about results at any level of the educational spectrum unnecessarily complicated. For example, take a minute and describe the similarities and differences among the following terms: achievement standard, behavioral objective, big idea, content standard, enduring understanding, essential knowledge, essential skill, grade-level expectation, knowledge standard, learning benchmark, learning target, performance objective, performance standard, primary objective, standard, and outcome.

DON'T ASK ME I DON'T KNOW

OZZY OSBOURNE • "I DON'T KNOW"

In light of this phenomenon, the underpinnings of forward thinking and consequential education are well deserving of clarification.

A.

By definition, a *goal* is one and the same as an *objective*.

⇕

n an aim or desired result (*goal*, def. 1)

⇕

n a thing aimed at or sought; a goal (*objective*, def. 1)

B.

The omnipresent goal/objective of education, in all contexts, in all subject areas, and at all grade levels, is to bring about *learning*. As the authors of the Faculty Development website for the College of Medicine at Florida State University (n.d.) illuminate, learning is one and the same as change:

> In educational psychology we define learning as a "change in behavior." This is a little confusing but if a student could not answer a particular question on a pretest, then received instruction, and then answered the question correctly on a posttest, a change in behavior is illustrated and learning is considered to have occurred. (§ 3, ¶ 1)

Edwards (1995) agrees:

> Education is directed by specified outcome expectations. These expectations refer to changes we desire to bring about in individuals in the school. We might expect such outcomes as adding to the knowledge students possess; organizing and strengthening students' values; improving the level of skill performance; or developing certain understandings, insights and appreciations. When these desired outcomes are expressed as a statement, we refer to them as educational goals. (p. 3)

ex·pec·ta·tion
n a standard of conduct or performance expected by or of somebody (often used in the plural) (*expectation*, def. 1)
n that which is expected or looked for (*expectation*, def. 2)

Thus, educational goals/objectives can be conceived as desired results in the form of *intended change* (Popham and Baker, 1970).

C.

The major form of change educators seek to bring about in learners involves *knowledge* and *skills*. Thus, the recurrent definition of "learning" makes perfect sense.

1. Knowledge – *Knowledge* and human power are synonymous (Francis Bacon, 1620, Aphorism 3). Accordingly and appropriately, knowledge is the foundation of most educational goals. In terms of distinguishing knowledge, "researchers have found that content knowledge, whether it be in mathematics, science, or any other subject, can be divided into two distinct types of knowledge: declarative knowledge and

learn·ing
n knowledge or skill acquired by instruction or study (*learning*, def. 1)
n the acquisition of knowledge or skills through experience, practice, study, or by being taught (*learning*, def. 2)
n the cognitive process of acquiring skill or knowledge (*learning*, def. 3)

procedural knowledge" (Paris and Lindauer and Paris, Lipson, and Wixson as cited in Marzano, Pickering, and McTighe, 1993, p. 16). These distinctions coincide with the "types of knowledge" included in *The Revised Bloom's Taxonomy* (Anderson and Krathwohl, eds., 2001): factual knowledge, conceptual knowledge, metacognitive knowledge, and procedural knowledge.

The authors of *The Revised Bloom's Taxonomy*—a team of cognitive psychologists, curriculum and instructional researchers, and testing and assessment specialists—describe factual knowledge as "bits of information," such as terms and facts, and conceptual knowledge as more complex and organized forms of knowledge (p. 46):

- Classifications and categories (e.g., periods of geological time, forms of business ownership)
- Principles and generalizations (e.g., Pythagorean theorem, law of supply and demand)
- Theories, models, and structures (e.g., theory of evolution, structure of Congress)

Factual and conceptual knowledge are sub-types of declarative knowledge, the medium through which people think and talk about the world (Clark, 2004).

20

> In cognitive psychology, declarative knowledge is usually defined in terms of "knowing that": *knowing that* Bogota is the capital of Colombia, or *knowing that* a square is a two-dimensional figure with four perpendicular sides of equal length. (Anderson et al, 2000, p. 41)

> [Declarative knowledge is] awareness and understanding of factual information about the world—*knowing that* in contrast to *knowing how*. Its necessary and sufficient conditions are that the information must be true, that the person must believe it to be true, and that the person must be in a position to know it. Typical items of declarative knowledge might include: that Princess Diana died in 1997; that Goethe was 83 when he finished writing *Faust*; that there is a village in Hertfordshire, England, called Ugley. (Colman, 2001, emphasis added)

Andrew knows that a chromatic scale has twelve pitches, each a half step apart.

Aaron knows that proper singing posture is relaxed and free of tension.

Angie knows that détaché is a bowing technique in which the performer plays one note per bow stroke, alternating between up-bows and down-bows.

Metacognitive knowledge is "knowledge of cognition in general as well as awareness and knowledge of one's own cognition" (Anderson, et al., 2000, p. 46). As learners acquire metacognitive knowledge, or become more aware of their thinking, they gain increased control over their learning. For example:

> Imagine a student studying for an exam. It is well past midnight, she has been studying for hours, and is exhausted. The decision that this student must make is whether she has studied the material for exam sufficiently and can go to sleep, or whether she must brew another pot of coffee and keep studying. The student must decide whether the material is generally well-learned, and if not, what information necessitates further study. (Perfect and Schwartz, 2002, p. 1)

Procedural knowledge is "know-how" (e.g., knowing how to ride a bicycle) or the knowledge that is exercised (used, applied), and therefore demonstrated, in the accomplishment of some task (Stillings, et al., 1995). Additional examples of procedural knowledge include performing long division, shooting free throws, editing a composition for mechanics, singing Italian arias, counting rhythms, improvising solos in the Blues style, or analyzing music for architectural form (adapted from Marzano, 2007).

21

Perhaps dissecting knowledge might seem unnecessary or even counterproductive within a profession that is far too abundant in terms that are frequently used but not fully understood. The value of even modest efforts, however, is far-reaching. As illustrated by Bennett Reimer, eminent music educator and authority on the philosophy of music education, "knowing about knowing" brings clarity to an essential perspective: consequential music education encompasses (requires!) multiple dimensions of knowledge.

Type of Knowledge	Dimensions of knowing that are implicated in musical experience (Reimer, 2008, p. 2):
Factual	***Knowing about*** = information apropos to performing, composing, arranging, improvising, listening, analyzing, evaluating, and understanding music in relation to its history and contexts.
Conceptual . . .	***Knowing why*** = infinite philosophical or theoretical understandings surrounding musical endeavors.
Procedural . . .	***Knowing how*** = the collective skills of the body, mind, and sensitivities that are required for creating music and for sharing the musical creations of others.
Metacognitive .	***Knowing within*** = the unification of music and self; an inner relationship with music that cannot be adequately described, yet is potent and very real.

2. Skill – Ask anyone who was ever skilled at anything, consult every dictionary of choice, or describe the performance of someone who is clearly competent. Either way, the same definition arises: a "skill" is *the ability to do something well*.

skill
n the ability to do something well; expertise (*skill*, def. 1)
n the ability to do something well, usually gained through training or experience (*skill*, def. 2)
n a learned power of doing something competently; a developed aptitude or ability (*skill*, def. 3)

From this distinction, there are two important points that follow. First, the heart of skill is *ability*—performing long division, shooting free throws, editing compositions for mechanics, singing Italian arias, counting rhythms, improvising solos in the Blues style, and analyzing scores for architectural form, for example, are all "somethings" that students can learn to do well or become "skilled" in doing; they are not "skills" in and of themselves. Second, a skill can be simple (e.g., a discrete procedure) or complex and multidimensional (e.g., a process or combination of skills). Either way, people learn to "do things well" by applying various types of knowledge. Without exception, and regardless of context or complexity, developing a skill involves knowledge in verbal/declarative, non-verbal/procedural, and metacognitive form:

Consider…persuasive writing as a desired achievement. At first blush, it would appear that we are dealing exclusively with a performance based on a set of straightforward skills to be learned through practice and feedback. But on further reflection, we note a key conceptual element here, something that must be understood apart from the particular writing skills. Students must come to an understanding of persuasion and how it works if their writing and speaking are to ever be truly persuasive. (Wiggins and McTighe, 2006, p. 77)

⟺

Consider…[artistic music-making] as a desired achievement. At first blush, it would appear that we are dealing exclusively with a performance based on a set of straightforward skills to be learned through practice and feedback. But on further reflection, we note a key conceptual element here, something that must be understood apart from the particular [performance] skills. Students must come to an understanding of [artistry]…if their [music-making is] to ever be truly [artistic]. (Wiggins and McTighe, 2006, p. 77)

learn
v to acquire knowledge or skill or a behavioral tendency (*learn*, def. 1)

D.

In addition to knowledge-based outcomes, and true to the definition of "learn," preparing students to navigate the world before them also involves *dispositions*—inclinations or tendencies to think or act in a particular way.

> The point of school is effective *use* of knowledge and skill in real situations. Content knowledge is a means, not the end. Ask yourself: what's the point of knowing a lot of content if you lack the habits and attitudes needed to use the content in new, challenging or problematic settings? An irony, of course, is that often teachers as well as parents fail to have the requisite habits of mind to develop those very habits in their kids—patience, persistence, openness to novelty, etc. (Wiggins, 2008, ¶ 8)

Carol S. Dweck (2000), professor of psychology, author, and recognized leader in the field of motivation, personality, and developmental psychology, further illuminates the value of productive dispositions:

> What has intrigued me most in my 30 years of research is the power of motivation. Motivation is often more important than initial ability in determining whether a person succeeds in the long run. In fact, many creative geniuses were not born that way. They were often fairly ordinary people who became extraordinarily motivated. By motivation, I mean not only the desire to achieve but also the love of learning, the love of challenge, and the ability to thrive on obstacles. *These are the greatest gifts we can give our students.* (p. 14, emphasis added)

Productive dispositions can be classified in two broad categories: habits of mind and habits of demeanor. According to Costa and Kallick (2000–01), a "habit of mind" means "having a disposition toward behaving intelligently when confronted with problems, the answers to which are not immediately known" (¶ 2). The habits of mind identified by Costa and Kallick include:

- Persisting
- Thinking and communicating with clarity and precision
- Managing impulsivity
- Gathering data through all senses
- Listening with understanding and empathy
- Creating, imagining, innovating
- Thinking flexibly
- Responding with wonderment and awe
- Thinking about thinking
- Taking responsible risks
- Striving for accuracy
- Finding humor
- Questioning and posing problems
- Thinking interdependently
- Applying past knowledge to new situations
- Remaining open to continuous learning

Habits of demeanor encompass behaviors that represent widespread human values, are central to achieving academic goals, and are essential to leading productive and fulfilling lives—prosocial behaviors that students should be inclined to demonstrate. The Josephson Institute's "Character Counts" program (initiated in 1993), for example, focuses on "Six Pillars of Character" (2008a):

- Trustworthiness (honesty, loyalty, reliability)
- Respect (consideration, courtesy/manners, peaceful conflict resolution)
- Responsibility (accountability, perseverance, self-control, self-discipline)
- Fairness (open-mindedness, playing by the rules, sharing)
- Caring (altruism, compassion, forgiveness, gratitude, kindness)
- Citizenship (contribution, cooperation, participation, patriotism, protection)

With these additions, the "intended change" we seek for learners—learning—is perhaps best described as the acquisition, integration, extension, or refinement of knowledge and dispositions [through study, experience, or by being taught] (Marzano, 1992). Naturally, if we want our students to be "smart but not arrogant, flexible but not easily deterred from their hopes and dreams, compassionate toward others but not overly accommodating, self-confident but not too preoccupied with themselves, proud but not exclusive" (San Antonio, 2006, p. 13), then goals throughout education—in every K–12 classroom—must include attitudes, perceptions, and mental habits that are central to "wellness."

True or False?

I want to make a difference in the lives of my students.

True or False?

To have made a difference, students must become different.

II

NO WIND SERVES HIM WHO ADDRESSES HIS VOYAGE

TO NO CERTAIN PORT.

—MICHEL DE MONTAIGNE

Regardless of subject matter, a more specific vision of an accomplished or changed learner evolves from standards. Educational standards represent a consensus of what parents, teachers, administrators, school boards, and community organizations believe is most important for students to learn and teachers to teach. In essence, standards clarify the most valuable and important outcomes of K–12 education. Thus, standards are in fact educational goals, or at the very least, the primary foundation for establishing goals.

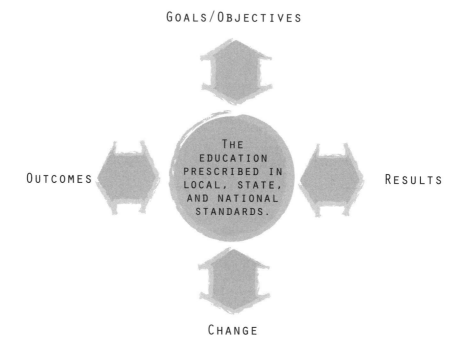

GOALS/OBJECTIVES

THE EDUCATION PRESCRIBED IN LOCAL, STATE, AND NATIONAL STANDARDS.

OUTCOMES

RESULTS

CHANGE

III.

YOU'VE GOT TO THINK ABOUT "BIG THINGS"
WHILE YOU'RE DOING SMALL THINGS,
SO THAT ALL THE SMALL THINGS
GO IN THE RIGHT
DIRECTION.
—ALVIN TOFFLER

In virtually all state and national standards publications, a distinct hierarchy exists. At the highest level are "exit-level" expectations—the ultimate outcomes of K–12 schooling. Broad and overarching in scope, these expectations generally appear in four distinct forms: (a) summative, (b) cross-curricular/cross-disciplinary, (c) domain-specific, and (d) discipline-specific.

A. Summative standards – A summative, exit-level expectation is a broad, overarching description of an accomplished learner after K–12 (or Pre-K–12) education is complete. For example, the Missouri *Show-Me Standards* (1996) are summarized as follows: "Graduates of Missouri's public schools [will] have the knowledge, skills, and competencies essential to leading productive, fulfilling and successful lives as they continue their education, enter the workforce, and assume their civic responsibilities" (Missouri Department of Elementary and Secondary Education, Overview of Performance Standards, ¶ 1).

B. Cross-curricular or cross-disciplinary standards – Cross-curricular standards in most state and national frameworks encompass overarching abilities, capacities, or processes that are central to reaching summative standards. To provide examples of exit-level, cross-disciplinary capacities, two 21st-century skill sets are particularly elucidatory.

28

1. The *enGauge 21st Century Skills: Literacy in the Digital Age* (North Central Regional Educational Laboratory and the Metiri Group, 2003) is a collection of standards that evolved through an exhausting process that included "literature reviews, research on emerging characteristics of the Net-Generation, a review of current reports on workforce trends from business and industry, analysis of nationally recognized skill sets, input from educators, data from educator surveys, and reactions from constituent groups" (p. 10). Additionally, "data was gathered from educators at state-level conference sessions in ten states, surveys, and focus groups in Chicago and Washington, DC. Initial drafts of the *enGauge 21st Century Skills* were reviewed by experts in the field prior to inclusion in the *enGauge* list" (p. 10).

2. The *Framework for 21st Century Learning* (2007) sets forth a vision for 21st-century student success in the global economy. This skill set is published by the Partnership for 21st Century Skills, a public-private advocacy organization with partners including the National Education Association.

The table shown on the next page merges skills from each publication, excluding goals/objectives that are specific to content areas (i.e., reading/language arts, math, science, arts). The result is a framework of life-supporting and -enriching abilities, or in terms of **Expectation**, examples of consequential exit-level, cross-disciplinary objectives.

C. *Domain-specific standards* – Domain-specific, exit-level standards are specific to a particular sphere of knowledge (e.g., math, science, or the arts). As students acquire, integrate, extend, and refine knowledge within the various domains, which is undeniably valuable in and of itself, they also move closer to achieving cross-disciplinary, exit-level goals.

Specific to the domain of art, the *National Standards for Arts Education* sets forth five broad capabilities that encompass what students should "know and be able to do by the time they have completed secondary school" (Consortium of National Arts Education Associations, 1994, Introduction, § 4, ¶ 7):

21st Century Skills

Framework for 21st Century Learning (Partnership for 21st Century Skills, 2007)	enGauge 21st Century Skills (NCREL and Metiri Group, 2003)	Generalizations The ability to:
Creativity and Improvisation	Curiosity, Creativity, and Risk Taking	Use knowledge meaningfully* (Marzano, 1992).
Critical Thinking and Problem Solving	Higher-Order Thinking and Sound Reasoning	
Communication	Interactive Communication	Communicate successfully.
Collaboration Social and Cross-Cultural Skills Global Awareness	Teaming, Collaboration, and Interpersonal Skills Multicultural Literacy and Global Awareness	Collaborate effectively.
Information Literacy	Information Literacy	Use technology proficiently. Accomplish quality results efficiently. Adapt to change fluidly.
Media Literacy	Visual Literacy	
Information, Communications, and Technology Literacy	Technological Literacy	
Productivity and Accountability	Prioritizing, Planning, and Managing for Results Effective Use of Real-World Tools Ability to Produce Relevant, High-Quality Products	
Initiative and Self-Direction	Self-Direction	Learn independently and strategically.
Leadership and Responsibility Civic Literacy	Personal, Social, and Civic Responsibility	Contribute to family, school, and community positively.

* "Using knowledge meaningfully" encompasses a host of essential skills, from decision making, investigation, experimental inquiry, problem solving, and invention (Marzano, Pickering, and McTighe, 1993) to the "Hidden Skills of Academic Literacy" (Strong, Silver, and Perini, 2001, p. 57):

- Analyzing and applying models and concepts
- Collecting and organizing ideas and information
- Conducting comparative analysis
- Constructing well-formed explanations
- Critiquing performance against set criteria
- Making reasonable inferences
- Planning effectively
- Reading and interpreting visual data
- Using abstract vocabulary
- Writing effectively about two or more readings
- Writing effectively in specific genres

[Students] should be able to communicate at a basic level in the four arts disciplines: dance, music, theatre, and the visual arts. This includes knowledge and skills in the use of the basic vocabularies, materials, tools, techniques, and intellectual methods of each arts discipline.

[Students] should be able to communicate proficiently in at least one art form, including the ability to define and solve artistic problems with insight, reason, and technical proficiency.

[Students] should be able to develop and present basic analyses of works of art from structural, historical, and cultural perspectives, and from combinations of those perspectives. This includes the ability to understand and evaluate work in the various arts disciplines.

[Students] should have an informed acquaintance with exemplary works of art from a variety of cultures and historical periods, and a basic understanding of historical development in the arts disciplines, across the arts as a whole, and within cultures.

[Students] should be able to relate various types of arts knowledge and skills within and across the arts disciplines. This includes mixing and matching competencies and understandings in art-making, history and culture, and analysis in any arts-related project.

D. Discipline-specific standards – Beyond the bricks, mortar, and bells of present-day schools, people listen to music, perform music, improvise music, compose music, arrange music, combine music with visual media, record (preserve) music, search for music, buy music, sell music, steal music, collect music, share music, watch music on televisions and computers, attend musical events, talk about music, write about music, read about music, and form deep, personal relationships with music. Notwithstanding the fact that "music" is equal to "songs, artists, and/or performances we like," this list captures musical behaviors that are recurrent, and therefore valued, outside of school. These behaviors are also the prime catalyst for casting musical goals to be achieved inside of schools. Logically, valuable music learning between the bells prepares students for valued musical doing beyond the bells. As a means to this end, consensus rises to the call. The Music Educators National Conference (MENC), which is now MENC: The National Association for Music Education, established the National Standards for Music Education in 1994 in conjunction with the National Standards for Arts Education. According to the MENC Task Force on National Standards (2007): "The core of the music Standards is summarized in nine Content Standards that encompass the major ways in which people interact with music in our culture" (¶ 2). Content Standards identify the "broad subject matter" (MENC, 1994, p. 2) that is of central or fundamental importance to the ultimate goal of music education: "to improve the quality of life for all students by developing their *capacities* to participate fully in their musical culture" (MENC, 1994, p. 2, emphasis added).

National Content Standards for Music Education, Grades K–12 (MENC, 1994)

1. Singing, alone and with others, a varied repertoire of music.
2. Performing on instruments, alone and with others, a varied repertoire of music.
3. Improvising melodies, variations, and accompaniments.
4. Composing and arranging music within specified guidelines.
5. Reading and notating music.
6. Listening to, analyzing, and describing music.
7. Evaluating music and music performances.
8. Understanding relationships between music, the other arts, and disciplines outside the arts.
9. Understanding music in relation to history and culture.

IV

THE HIDDEN HARMONY IS BETTER THAN THE OBVIOUS.

—PABLO PICASSO

Implicit to all exit-level standards, including music, are two overarching concepts with far-reaching application to the formation of exit-level goals.

A. *Capacity without quality runs counter to educational aims with lasting value and consequence.* Capacity with quality, however, is skill—the ability to do something well. Regardless of grade level or subject matter, mediocrity has no place in meaningful education.

B. *Capacity without flexibility runs counter to educational aims with lasting value and consequence.* Anything understood in only one way is not really understood. Someone who is clearly knowledgeable about a topic or subject is someone who can transfer knowledge effectively to new problems and settings. In other words, someone who clearly "understands" is someone who has "the ability to think and act flexibly with what one knows" or "flexible performance capability with emphasis on the flexibility" (Perkins as cited in Wiske, 1998, p. 40).

…understanding a topic of study is a matter of being able to perform in a variety of thought-demanding ways with the topic, for instance to: explain, muster evidence, find examples, generalize, apply concepts, analogize, represent in a new way, and so on…The more thought-demanding performances the student can display, the more confident we would be that the student understands. (Perkins, 1993, ¶19)

[Understanding] is typically manifested through performances involving one or more of the six facets of understanding. (Wiggins and McTighe, 2006, p. 126)

Teaching for understanding aims at having students explain, interpret, and apply, while showing insight from perspective, empathy, and self-knowledge. (Wiggins and McTighe, 1998, p. 64)

The same concept holds true with capacity. Someone who is clearly capable is someone who is versatile and adaptive. For example, just because Marissa can correctly identify the form of the first movement of Beethoven's Fifth Symphony doesn't mean she is proficient at identifying musical forms, or simply because Marcus performs a solo in a captivating manner doesn't mean he is an accomplished performer. Thus, in terms of exit-level goals, an essential characteristic of capacity is not only the ability to do something well but also the ability to do that "something" well in contexts of diverse structure and sophistication. Bob Dylan says it best: "There is nothing so stable as change."

V

GOALS ARE DISCOVERED, NOT MADE.

—RICHARD J. FOSTER

By applying the factors of quality and flexibility to the K–12 National Content Standards for Music Education (MENC, 1994), the results are something of immense importance to educators: exit-level goals that glow with lasting value and consequence.

> **National Content Standard 1**: Singing, alone and with others, a varied repertoire of music.
>
> **National Content Standard 2**: Playing on instruments, alone and with others, a varied repertoire of music.
> ⇕
> In contexts of diverse structure and sophistication, the students will be able to perform music artistically.

As one of mankind's oldest, most intimate, and basic forms of communication and cultural expression (Colorado Department of Education, 1997), performing music via voice or instrument is a cornerstone of music education by any standard or perspective. Performing music is "presenting or demonstrating an existing [musical composition], informally or formally; a process that calls upon the technical, expressive, and interpretive skills of the learner" (North Carolina Department of Public Instruction, 2000, Music: Strands: Performing).

This thing we call "music-making" has the incredible power to change lives. Whether it's through our performances, or our instruction, or the wonderful discipline that this art form engenders in people, the process of music-making has made our world a better, richer place because of the way it shapes us as people. (Chung, 2001, p. 26)

Performing music "artistically" aims at performance that is characteristic of art and artists; an artistic performance represents (respects, honors, reflects) objective, subjective, and contextual conventions of quality in relation to timbre (qualities of sound), pitch (frequencies of sound), duration (movement of sound), and intensity (volume of sound). "Contexts of diverse structure and sophistication" naturally encompasses performing, alone and with others, a varied repertoire of music.

National Content Standard 4: Composing and arranging music within specified guidelines.

⇕

In contexts of diverse structure and sophistication, the students will be able to create music effectively.

Creating music encompasses all types of original work including, but far from limited to, composing in traditional forms, converting music from one medium to another, and constructing dynamic audio/visual compositions with state-of-the-art technology. Creating music "effectively" aims at creating music in a way that produces a *desired result*—music that satisfies a requirement, communicates an idea, meets a certain guideline, serves a specific purpose, or achieves a desired effect.

What about National Content Standard 3: Improvising melodies, variations, and accompaniments? "Indigenous music of every culture was first improvised and then passed on to subsequent generations through aural or rote learning. Improvisation continues to be an important means of self-expression in all cultures and is an integral part of students' musical heritage" (Wisconsin Department of Public Instruction, 1997, p. 8). In addition to its musical value, improvisation is an opportunity for students to exercise creative thinking in unmatched form. Within the context of overarching, exit-level goals, however, improvisation (or creating and performing music simultaneously and spontaneously) is subsumed within the goals of performing music artistically and creating music effectively.

36

National Content Standard 5: Reading and notating music.

In contexts of diverse structure and sophistication, the students will be able to read and notate music proficiently.

Music notation is an historic, cross-cultural system of communication. Accordingly, learning to read and write this notation gives students access to centuries of wisdom and artistic expression from throughout the globe. Although music reading is often taught in conjunction with other types of musical doing, particularly performing, reading is a distinct capacity in and of itself. Reading music, as in looking at musical symbols and interpreting the information conveyed by the symbols, either internally (silently, mentally) or externally (communicating via voice or instrument), is "speaking" the language of music. In contrast, to "perform" is to carry out an action, accomplish a task, do what is required, present something, or function in a particular way or to a particular standard. Both are, of course, extremely relevant to music performers, but they are not one and the same—reading music proficiently, or even expertly, does not necessarily translate as performing music artistically. The complexities and refinements inherent to a genuinely artistic performance are the results of time, practice, effort, insight, emotion, dedication, maturity, repetition…and the list goes on and on. Reading well reduces the time required to reach an artistic level of performance, but genuine artistry, particularly at the K–12 level, rarely occurs "at sight." Furthermore, people who cannot read music can, do, and will continue to perform in a very artistic manner. In essence, the combined goals of performing artistically and reading proficiently is teaching and learning how to solve (achieve an artistic level of performance; artistically perform) musical problems (exercises, etudes, excerpts, solos, and parts) without the assistance of others, or developing artistic independence as a music performer.

National Content Standard 6: Listening to, analyzing, and describing music.

⇕

In contexts of diverse structure and sophistication, the students will be able to analyze and describe music accurately.

An analysis is an examination of the elements or structure of something—dealing with parts and wholes (Anderson, 2005). As defined by MENC (1994), elements of music—the parts that form musical wholes—include "pitch, rhythm, harmony, dynamics, timbre, texture, and form" (p. 41). Although the ability to analyze music is similar to other types of musical action, it is significant in and of itself. For example, a person who can read something may not be able to analyze it well. Similarly, someone who can analyze something may evaluate it poorly (Anderson, et al., 2001). Describing music, which almost always is based on some form of analysis, encompasses the ability to give correct or truthful accounts, representation, or explanations of music in verbal, non-verbal, objective, and/or subjective form.

What about listening to music? Listening, which is a far cry from "hearing," is a form of responding to music that is central to significant accomplishment in any musical capacity. Ironically, listening is also the only type of response that is largely intangible by itself. In combination with other forms of musical action, however, the story changes dramatically. A coherent evaluation of a live concert, a score that is free of errors, or a trio performing with exemplary intonation, for example, are tangible expressions of mature or maturing listening skills.

National Content Standard 7: Evaluating music and music performances.

⇕

In contexts of diverse structure and sophistication, the students will be able to evaluate music and music performances coherently.

co·her·ent
adj logically or aesthetically ordered or integrated (*coherent*, def. 1)

Learning to evaluate music and music performances coherently is learning to construct critical responses that are well reasoned and/or reflective of personal musical penchants. An accomplished critical thinker about music creates credible and coherent judgments for or against music and music performances by combining information gathered from listening and/or analysis and comparing it to personal, universal, subjective, and objective *conventions of quality*.

> As students gain the ability to develop and apply specific criteria for judging and evaluating the quality and effectiveness of music and performances, they are better able to apply criteria to improving their own work, realizing that the same criteria may not apply to music from other cultures and time periods. They also gain insights into why and how people from different parts of the world create and respond to music. (California Department of Education, 2004, p. 104)

In terms of traditional and contemporary compositions, arrangements, and transcriptions—musical inventions—conventions of quality are the customary ways in which music is created within a particular genre or style. The term "genre" denotes a type or category of music that shares common characteristics in broad ways (e.g., opera); the term "style" denotes music that shares common characteristics in more specific ways (e.g., bluegrass). For music performance, conventions of quality differ, either slightly or dramatically, among genres and styles, and are equivalent to the customary ways in which components of artistic performance are presented or carried out.

Evaluation has wide-ranging applications and value throughout the musical world. For example, people buy music, download music, and share music based on evaluation; people edit compositions and arrangements based on evaluation; people win concerto competitions, earn chairs in an orchestra, or secure contracts based on evaluation; and the combined actions of listening, analyzing, describing, and evaluating is the means by which most people educate themselves about music.

National Content Standard 8: Understanding relationships between music, the other arts, and disciplines outside the arts.
National Content Standard 9: Understanding music in relation to history and culture.
⇕
In contexts of diverse structure and sophistication, the students will be able to relate music meaningfully.

"Music is an important element of the historical and cultural record of humankind" (Colorado Department of Education, 1997, p. 9). Accordingly, music is an important means by which students can learn about the world. National Content Standards 8 and 9 underscore this premise by emphasizing important associative understandings, specifically, the ability to perceive and explain the meaning or the nature of associations between music and art, history, culture, and disciplines outside of the arts. To further "understand" (*v*) these target "understandings" (*n*), it is helpful to consider the verbs that are listed in the Achievement Standards for National Content Standards 8 and 9: "cite, classify, compare, demonstrate, describe, explain, identify, and trace" (MENC, 1994, p. 20). By citing, classifying, comparing, demonstrating, describing, explaining, identifying, and tracing various aspects of music in relation to art, history, culture, and disciplines outside of the arts, students develop and demonstrate musical understanding in relation to art, history, culture, and disciplines outside of the arts. Equally, these actions are examples of ways in which people *relate*—to find or show connections between [something] and [something else]. Thus, the ability to relate music comprehensively is the ability to find and show connections between music and art, history, culture, disciplines outside of the arts, and self. Because music is simultaneously personal and global, associative understanding is incomplete without attention to music's personal meaning and relevance. Regardless of context, relating music *meaningfully* is straightforward: making connections that have a serious, important, or useful quality or purpose.

In sum, the capacity to organize, manipulate, and construct meaning from sounds is a very real part of being human. It's also a very real part of a complete 21st-century education.

Synergy

Summative Standards	Example: Students will be able to lead productive, fulfilling, and successful lives as they continue their education, enter the workforce, and assume their civic responsibilities.	
Cross-Disciplinary Standards/ Process Standards	⇧ 21st-Century Skills	⇧ Productive Dispositions

Domain-Specific Content Standards	⇧ ***Arts***	⇧ *Comm. Arts*	⇧ *Health/PE*	⇧ *Math*	⇧ *Sciences*	⇧ *Social Studies*

National Standards for Arts Education
(Consortium of National Arts Education Associations, 1994)

Discipline-Specific Content Standards	⇧ *Dance*	⇧ ***Music***	⇧ *Theatre*	⇧ *Visual Arts*

National Content Standards for Music Education, Grades K-12 (MENC, 1994) ⇔ In contexts of diverse structure and sophistication, the students will be able to…

1. Singing, alone and with others, a varied repertoire of music.

…perform music artistically.

2. Performing on instruments, alone and with others, a varied repertoire of music.

⇕

…create music effectively.

3. Improvising melodies, variations, and accompaniments.

⇕

…read and notate music proficiently.

4. Composing and arranging music within specified guidelines.

⇕

5. Reading and notating music.

…analyze and describe music accurately.

6. Listening to, analyzing, and describing music.

⇕

7. Evaluating music and music performances.

…evaluate music and music performances coherently.

8. Understanding relationships between music, the other arts, and disciplines outside the arts.

⇕

…relate music meaningfully.

9. Understanding music in relation to history and culture.

VI

True or False?

There are many ways to be musical.

Exit-level objectives derived from the K–12 National Content Standards for Music (MENC, 1994) encompass something very special that all musicians share in common. To one degree or another, anyone who is musically educated possesses a distinct attribute: musicianship.

"Musicianship" is an elusive term that is most often connected to music performers. For example, in the Cambridge Advanced Learner's Dictionary, "musicianship" is defined as "a person's skill in playing a musical instrument or singing." In terms of semantics, however, the composition of this term radiates much more. The core of the word without any affixes is "music." The suffixes "-ian" and "-ship" add the following:

"Musicianship" Defined

	-ian	-ship
The New Oxford American Dictionary	*suffix* forming adjectives and nouns such as Christian (*-ian*, def. 1)	*suffix forming nouns* denoting a quality or condition; denoting a skill in a certain capacity (*-ship*, def. 1)
Merriam-Webster Online Dictionary	*noun suffix* one skilled in or specializing in (*-ian*, def. 2)	*noun suffix* state; condition; quality; art; skill (*-ship*, def. 2)

From the analysis shown above, the term "musicianship" denotes a skilled musician or *skill as a musician,* which is far from exclusive. As revealed in virtually every set of music standards in existence, there are three modes of musical action or three overarching ways in which to be *a musician*. The American School Band Directors Association (1997), for example, categorizes musical action as follows: "Musical processes include creating (composing and improvising), performing (playing, singing, conducting), and responding (listening, moving, analyzing, critiquing)" (p. 104). Thus, musicianship encompasses skill in any mode of musical action— performing music, creating music, or responding to music. And since the exit-level objectives derived from the National Content Standards are inter-related macro-skills, logic suggests that *comprehensive and adaptive musicianship* is (a) the ability to perform, create, and respond to music competently within contexts of diverse structure and sophistication, and (b) the pathway to exit-level arts education goals within the discipline of music.

Musicianship: *skill* as a musician.

⇕

n the ability to *do something well*

⇓

perform music artistically
create music effectively
read and notate music proficiently
analyze and describe music accurately
evaluate music and music
    performances coherently
relate music meaningfully

43

VII

SCHOOL MATTERS, BUT ONLY INSOFAR AS IT YIELDS SOMETHING THAT CAN BE USED ONCE STUDENTS LEAVE SCHOOL.

—HOWARD GARDNER

Consequential music education does not take shape *in vacuo*, by whim, or through personal agenda. Nor does it stem exclusively from previous experience. Music education that outlives school evolves from reasoning, reality, consensus, and usefulness as multi-functional capacities that empower students to navigate harmoniously through the multi-musical experience known as life. To put it another way, if the ultimate aim of schooling is to equip students for fluid and effective performance in the world (Wiggins and McTighe, 2006), and if the concomitant, ultimate aim of music education is "to improve the quality of life for all students by developing their capacities to participate fully in their musical culture" (MENC, 1994, p. 2), then the goals embedded in the National Standards are bursting with lasting value and consequence. By cultivating comprehensive and adaptive musicianship, even at its roots or earliest stages, music educators pay forward capacities that are extremely useful in several inter-reliant ways. This applies to all learners, regardless of age, gender, culture, language, race/ethnicity, socioeconomic status, or special abilities/disabilities.

A. Musicianship is a transmitter—fuel for self-expression. An artistic performance or creation of music, regardless of complexity, is the effect of (the result of) applying musicianship. Additionally, when one speaks intelligently about music or makes an informed judgment about a music performance, musicianship is the driving force.

B. Musicianship is a receiver, a filter for constructing meaning from sounds. As musicianship matures, so does one's ability to *"listen for"* music (Elliot, 1995, p. 99), which is a wonderful world away from *listening to*, or merely *hearing,* music.

> ...whether we like it or not, all music—good, bad, old, new, simple, complex, loud, soft—is contextually friendly, seemingly bent on soaking up whatever is around it, easily shifting from foreground to background. It takes a special effort of the aesthetic will to keep it in the foreground—to encounter it on its own terms and for its inherent worth—even when we consciously devote ourselves to this task. (Best, 1995, § 1, ¶ 6)

Do you remember department recitals? As a freshman, do you recall sitting through seemingly endless performances of *zingen owf Doych* and (silently) wondering why that person was working so hard to bore you? If so, perhaps your receiver wasn't tuned to their channel. With time, practice(!), and experience, however, did you reach a point where you could construct meaning from virtually any foreign musical experience?

As musicianship matures, students become more acute at constructing meaning from all kinds of music by "seeing all there is to see," which may very well be hidden to others.

> Beauty exists only in relation to a responsive subject; it must appear beautiful to someone…In appreciating beauty, we admire that which deserves to be admired. To cultivate taste is therefore to cultivate judgment. Beauty, in short, is in the eye of the *educated* beholder. (Kalkavage, 2006, § 5, ¶ 2)

45

C. The pursuit of musicianship is the link between people and the rewards of musical action. As Saunders (2004) suggests, by delving deeply into music, there is much to be gleaned about the human condition, the personal meaning(s) that music evokes, and how meaning can be transformed by the "mere act of listening and the circumstances in which this act takes place" (p. 65). Furthermore, by working to read notes and rhythms as well as letters and words, or to uncover hidden dimensions of a particular repertoire, or to bring an original musical idea to life with technology, for example, opportunities abound in relation to a host of human rewards. Enjoyment, recognition, remuneration, attention, awards, self-confidence, self-understanding, or even fame are all within reach of the steadfast musician.

D. Musicianship is a bonding agent. Whether at a concert, in a classroom, in an online discussion group, or through casual conversation at a book-music-video-coffee shop, even people with modest degrees of musicianship can connect with others who "breathe the same air." From the music of Indy's to the music of India, music brings people together. With so many forces in the world working to tear people apart, perhaps the connective power inherent to music, which is only magnified through the pursuit of musicianship, is something to seriously consider.

E. Finally, the pursuit of musicianship is a gateway, an entrance to lessons beyond compare. Perhaps music's greatest gift is potential. Music shares without condition or cause, willingly meshing with the life of whoever calls. And as every well-traveled musician knows, the experience can be life enriching, or perhaps life changing, from even a slight encounter. Thus, in many ways music is its own greatest teacher. Mere humans can teach others *how* to perform, create, or respond to music, but we pale in comparison to music itself when it comes to teaching *why*.

GLEN OF GUINNESS • "SONG OF THE SONGS"

PRÉCIS

MORE IMPORTANT THAN THE QUEST FOR

CERTAINTY

IS THE QUEST FOR

CLARITY.

—FRANCOIS GA

About a decade after graduating from college, I received news that a former teacher from my years in high school had taken ill. This was no ordinary teacher. He was a mentor, a consummate musician, an exemplary educator, and the inspiration for many(!) students to pursue a career in music education. Needless to say, I soon made my way to see him.

The magnitude of this visit was completely unexpected. Amid the reminiscing, the small talk, and the "shop talk," he somehow managed to inspire me yet again. Seemingly out of the blue, he said, "I hear you're very successful." Then after a long and somewhat awkward pause, he continued with words that would change my thinking forever. In a calm but raspy tone, and with genuine curiosity, he asked, "What are you succeeding at?"

Answering this equally monumental and disturbing question—forming a clear, guiding perspective of the ultimate goals, roles, and potential of music education—*is* the journey of **Expectation**.

QUESTIONS FOR REFLECTION

- What are my beliefs about the fundamental purposes of music education?
- Why should other people adopt my beliefs?
- How does my philosophy glow with lasting value and consequence?

destination: transformation

THERE ARE PAINTERS WHO TRANSFORM THE SUN INTO A YELLOW SPOT,

BUT THERE ARE OTHERS WHO,

THANKS TO THEIR ART AND INTELLIGENCE,

TRANSFORM A YELLOW SPOT INTO THE SUN.

—PABLO PICASSO

Think of someplace you would like to take your students. Any place will do. Just make sure that it's far away and important to you. The next step is obvious: Plan a course to get there. Before tackling this charge, however, be sure to factor in three prerequisite conditions. First, the point of departure will be different for each student. Second, you have a fixed window of limited time to get everyone there. Third, the most efficient mode of travel will vary from student to student. Some will require a nonstop flight; others will need to walk.

Regardless of subject matter, this is the challenge teachers face every day. Using the time we are given to advance each learner as far as possible toward consequential destinations is *sine qua non* of exemplary practice. You guessed it. Engineering such a feat—becoming expert at designing pathways that lead to the ultimate aims of music education—is also the journey of ***Transformation***.

So how does comprehensive and adaptive musicianship evolve? What does an effective course of action look like? This seems like a logical point of inquiry, particularly if we are genuinely concerned with enriching lives through music. Should students simply perform, create, read, notate, analyze, describe, evaluate, and relate music over and over again? Or is there more to it? The answer to both of these questions is a resounding yes!

I

LEARNING IS NOT ATTAINED BY CHANCE;

IT MUST BE SOUGHT FOR WITH ARDOR AND DILIGENCE.

—ABIGAIL ADAMS

(LETTER TO JOHN ADAMS, MAY 8, 1780)

Consequential music education requires systematic, sustained study. As June M. Hinckley, former president of MENC, remarked before the Subcommittee on Early Childhood, Youth and Families of the House Committee on Education and the Workforce:

> The research clearly shows that music instruction, taught by qualified teachers, produces measurable enhancements in the development of children's brains, resulting in significant educational benefits. It is important to note, however, that the cognitive and academic improvements highlighted by the research come about only with sequential instruction in music provided by qualified teachers, not through mere exposure to music. (1999, Implications for Education Reform, ¶ 1)

Time and again, music educators are reminded that a *program of study* is requisite to achieve the education set forth in the National Standards.

> All basic subjects, including the arts, require more than mere "exposure" or access. They need focused time for sequential study, practice, and reflection. (Consortium of National Arts Education Associations, 1994, Introduction, § 8, ¶ 1)

Because of the role of the arts in civilization, and because of their unique ability to communicate the ideas and emotions of the human spirit, every American student, preK through grade 12, should receive a balanced, comprehensive, sequential, and rigorous program of instruction in music and the other arts. (MENC, 1997, Where We Stand: The Role of Music in American Education: Access to Music Education, no. 1)

Effective arts education requires sequential curricula, regular time-on-task, qualified teachers, and a fair share of educational resources… arts instruction should be carried out with the same academic rigor and high expectations as instruction in other core subjects. (MENC, 1999, ¶ 6)

II

THE ROAD LEADING TO A GOAL DOES NOT SEPARATE YOU
FROM THE DESTINATION;
IT IS ESSENTIALLY A PART OF IT.
—CHARLES DE LINT, AUTHOR AND CELTIC FOLK MUSICIAN

Logically, to reach a faraway destination travelers must reach a series of sub-destinations, passing multiple milestones and guideposts along the way. *Comparatively,* to achieve the ultimate aims of music education (faraway destinations), students must complete units of study (milestones) and participate fully in lessons or rehearsals (guideposts) to pass grade levels or courses (sub-destinations). *Structurally,* this is the prototypical architecture of a program of study in today's schools; lessons or rehearsals, units, and grade levels or courses are the architectural structures in which sequential education is generally organized and delivered. *Effectively,* objectives are building blocks for creating these structures. *Thankfully,* conceiving a program of study as objectives at varying levels brings much-needed clarity, consistency, and straightforwardness to educational structure and design.

Exit-Level Objectives
⇧
Grade-Level or Course-Level Objectives
⇧
Unit-Level Objectives
⇧
Lesson-Level or Rehearsal-Level Objectives

III

THE JOURNEY OF A THOUSAND MILES BEGINS
WITH A SINGLE STEP.

—LAO TZU

In the journey to reach exit-level knowledge and dispositions (the ultimate aims of a program of study), a practical "single step" is analogous to a unit of study. A unit is a specific period of time, ranging from a few days to a few weeks, devoted to the achievement of one or more objectives that define the unit.

⇔

Within the prototypical architecture of K–12 schools, a grade level or course is a period of study devoted to achieving a series of unit-level objectives. Accordingly, a course-level objective is (should be) a summation of one or more unit-level objectives. By successfully achieving a unit-level objective, the learner demonstrates partial or complete achievement of one or more grade-level or course-level objectives.

IV

OUR ARCHITECTURE REFLECTS TRULY AS A MIRROR.

—LOUIS HENRI SULLIVAN

53

A series of units creates a pathway—a route that can lead to somewhere important or, on the other hand, to nowhere in particular. To achieve the education prescribed in the National Standards for Music Education (MENC, 1994), the units that define grade levels and courses must ultimately serve to develop and demonstrate comprehensive and adaptive musicianship. In support of such design, analysis of state and national achievement standards (see Appendix A) illuminates several important anchors. "Achievement standards," which are also known as "proficiency objectives," "grade-level expectations" (GLEs), or "course-level expectations" (CLEs), specify benchmarks of achievement at select junctures in a program of study.

A. Six overarching objectives are subsumed in the nine National Content Standards (as described in *Destination: Expectation*)**.** In state and national achievement standards, however, this number is effectively condensed to five. Reading music is subsumed in performing music; notating music is subsumed in creating music (see Appendix A, Tables 4 and 5). This is no small detail. Collectively, units of study must serve to develop and demonstrate musicianship through five mutually reinforcing pathways—a tall but suddenly manageable order:

Destination	Comprehensive Musicianship				
	⬈	⬈	⬆	⬊	⬊
Pathways	Performing music artistically (+ reading music proficiently)	Creating music effectively (+ notating music proficiently)	Analyzing and describing music accurately	Evaluating music and music performance coherently	Relating music meaningfully
	Performing	Creating	Responding		

HOLD TIGHT TO THE PATH YOU'RE WALKING

DON'T LET YOUR RESOLVE DECLINE

KEEP YOUR EYE ON THE PRIZE AND YOUR MIND ON YOUR GOALS

AND NEVER FALL BEHIND

VIER FACTOR I • "DREAM YOURSELF AWAKE"

B. The cornerstones of musicianship are complex and multidimensional, but not mysterious. With the addition of implicit quality indicators, benchmarks that are frequent in state and national achievement standards bring objective clarity to skills that are basic or fundamental to the macro-skills of musicianship. For example, according to consensus the ability to [correctly] identify musical forms, elements of music, instruments, various genres and styles of music, voice types, rhythmic elements, repetitions and contrasts, and compositional techniques are important skills that develop and demonstrate the ability to analyze and describe music accurately (see Appendix A).

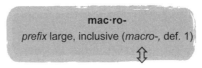

mac·ro-
prefix large, inclusive (*macro-*, def. 1)

True or False?

Core skills merge to create macro-skills.

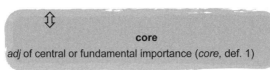

core
adj of central or fundamental importance (*core*, def. 1)

C. Recurrent benchmarks in state and national achievement standards often appear throughout the spectrum of grade levels. This phenomenon underscores the fact that skill—as in the ability to do something *well*—evolves incrementally.

> *Lasting change doesn't happen overnight. Lasting change happens in infinitesimal increments: a day, an hour, a minute, a heartbeat at a time.*
> —Sarah Ban Breathnach

Benchmarks that appear throughout the grade levels also underscore an important pathway to comprehensive and adaptive musicianship: introducing, integrating, extending, and refining core musical abilities through challenges that become increasingly diverse and sophisticated.

> Learning to perform, discuss or analyze only a few pieces of music well is not the same as learning a skill or knowledge…skills and knowledge will be acquired only when students have frequent opportunities to practice, when practice is efficient, and when practice involves numerous and varied examples in a motivating environment. (Jellison, 2000, p. 127)

> When learning a new skill, it's not until students have practiced upwards of about 24 times that they reach 80 percent competency (Marzano, Pickering, and Pollack, 2001, p. 67) [and the results of practice will be] increments in learning that start out rather large but gradually get smaller and smaller as students fine-tune their knowledge and skill. (Marzano, Pickering, and Pollock, 2001, pp. 68–69)

> Learning occurs through the growth of neural connections, stimulated by the passage of electrical current along nerve cells and enhanced by chemicals discharged into the synapse between neighboring cells. The more often the "trail is blazed," the more automatic a task or memory becomes (Buchell, Coull, and Friston, 1999). Therefore, the more a student repeats a learning task, the greater the connectivity. (Hardiman, 2001, p. 53)

> Nothing flies more in the face of the last 20 years of research than the assertion that practice is bad. All evidence, from the laboratory and from extensive case studies of professionals, indicates that real competence only comes with extensive practice…In denying the critical role of practice one is denying children the very thing they

need to achieve real competence. (Anderson, Reder, and Simon, 2000, Constructivism: ¶ 14)

Growth in singing and playing music occurs by applying skills to increasingly challenging music literature. (Colorado Model Content Standards for Music, 1997, p. 3)

Learning to play or sing any scale, any exercise, or any piece is never the real goal of music instruction, even though teachers may sometimes verbalize that these are their goals. The real goal—the meaningful, substantive, far-reaching goal—is for students to become superb musicians, doing all of the things that superb musicians do, irrespective of what is being played or sung [or analyzed, arranged, read, evaluated, etc.] at the moment. These far-reaching goals for music instruction do not change from lesson to lesson, rehearsal to rehearsal, week to week. The far-reaching goals remain the same *from the first day of instruction* to the time when the student reaches the highest levels of artistic musicianship. In this sense, the goals in the lesson plan never change, regardless of the skill or experience level of the students you're teaching. Only the contexts in which the goals are taught (i.e., the activities, the music) change over time. (Duke, 2005, pp. 30–31)

For example, by conquering "improvising" challenges that become increasingly diverse and sophisticated, a host of core abilities associated with performing music artistically, creating music effectively, and evaluating music performances coherently, at a minimum, are introduced, integrated, extended, and refined. By conquering "performing" challenges that become increasingly diverse and sophisticated, a host of core abilities associated with performing music artistically, reading music proficiently, and evaluating music performances coherently are introduced, integrated, extended, and refined. Of course, this is just scratching the surface. Depending on the architecture and complexity of a musical challenge, a multitude of core abilities could come into play. As Whitehead (1929) advised many moons ago, "Let the main ideas which are introduced into a child's education be few and important, and let them be thrown into every combination possible" (p. 2).

D. Something essential to all music classrooms is patently absent in most if not all publications that set forth standards.

> The Standards say nothing about what curricular materials or what repertoire should be used…These matters are up to the states, local school districts, and individual teachers. (MENC Task Force on National Standards, 2007, ¶ 23)

The absence of artists, composers, concepts, elements, facts, genres, literature, procedures, processes, relationships, styles, techniques, themes, topics, traditions, etc., reinforces a cornerstone of standards-based music education: content is a means, not an aim (Wiggins and McTighe, 1998/2006).

> Focusing on skill development rather than content coverage not only reorients teachers' priorities about the use of precious instructional time, but also reorients students' perceptions of what's important, what's deserving of their attention and effort, and what it means to be competent. (Duke, 2005, p. 80)

Although standards do not prescribe specific content, there is a distinct, implicit requirement: collectively, the literature selected for study, resource, or performance must meet three criteria.

Did you know? At all grade levels, in broad or specific form, Curriculum Maps can be used to delineate unit-level content. For example:

Grade Level: 3

Organizational Unit	Content
August	American Folk Songs
September	Dances
October	Nature Songs
November	Patriotic Music
December	Holiday Music around the World
January	Orchestral Music; The Symphony
February	Music of [prominent composer]
March	World Music; Music from [culture]
April	Song Stories
May	Music for Celebrations

First, and obviously, all literature should be appropriately gauged to the developmental stage of the learner.

Second, the music explored in the classroom should be diverse in scope. Students can learn much about the world by exploring the music of cultures other than their own. The authors of *The School Music Program: A New Vision* (MENC, 1994) bring this proposition into bright light:

> The music studied should reflect the multimusical diversity of America's pluralistic culture. It should include a broad range of genres, styles, and periods, including music from outside the art music tradition, music from the various cultures and ethnic groups that comprise American society, and authentic examples from the various musical cultures of the world. Many communities and many schools themselves are already smaller versions of the global village. The school music program should reflect that fact. (pp. 3–4)

Third, literature must be exemplary. Through the brilliance of exceptional artists, the impact of "curricular materials" can be nothing short of a triple blessing: musical growth, musical achievement, and the captivating experience that only comes from encounters with genuine works of art. DeRoche (2002) captures the veracity of this premise with great clarity: "It is not possible for people in any stage of development to have a significant response to insignificant music" (p. 19). Fortunately, from chant to rap, from samba to soul, and from musical practices around the globe, a wealth of life-changing, mood-swinging, perspective-stirring, and storytelling repertoire has never been more accessible.

In sum, standards-based music education is simultaneously finite and infinite. As long as the units that define a program of study serve to introduce, integrate, extend, or refine core musical skills, musicianship can be effectively developed and demonstrated through diverse, exemplary, and developmentally appropriate content of any color.

Performing Music

Pathway	[see Appendix A, Tables 1 and 2]		
	The student is able to perform…	*when singing or playing…*	
	expressively	music at an appropriate or specific level of difficulty.	nursery rhymes.
	with appropriate intonation		folk songs.
	with others; in an ensemble	independent parts (within an ensemble).	parts in a school musical.
	with appropriate dynamics		
	with technical accuracy	a varied repertoire.	exercises in method books.
	with appropriate posture		
	with appropriate phrasing	melodic patterns.	parts in large ensembles (concert and contest music).
	with characteristic tone quality	repertoire in a variety of genres and styles	
	with accurate rhythm		music for classroom recitals.
	with proper breath support	music written in two or more parts.	christmas carols in the town square.
	independently; alone		
	with a steady beat	rhythmic patterns. ⇔	parts in small ensembles.
	from memory		
	with appropriate blend	unaccompanied music.	solos.
	with appropriate balance	accompanied music.	improvisations.
	accurately		
	with well-developed ensemble skills	rhythmic patterns melodic, or harmonic patterns.	audition etudes for honor groups.
	with stylistic accuracy	accompaniments.	multi-movement, accompanied solos.
	by ear		
	with sensitivity to performance practices	harmonic patterns; harmonic progressions.	audition music for concerto competitions.
	with appropriate interpretation		etc.
		ostinatos.	
		rounds.	
		music in different languages.	
		etc.	
Destination	In contexts of diverse structure and sophistication, the students will be able to perform music artistically and read music proficiently. ⇕ National Content Standards for Music, Grades K–12 (MENC, 1994) • Singing, alone and with others, a varied repertoire of music. • Performing on instruments, alone and with others, a varied repertoire of music. • Reading music. ⇕ National Standards for Arts Education (Consortium of National Arts Education Association, 1994, Introduction, § 4, ¶ 7) • [Students] should be able to communicate proficiently in at least one art form, including the ability to define and solve artistic problems with insight, reason, and technical proficiency.		

Creating Music

Pathway	[see Appendix A, Table 4] *The student is able to…*	*when creating…*
	meet specific, teacher-specified compositional or arranging guidelines, e.g., the composition or arrangement: • attracts interest upon first hearing; possesses memorable qualities; is clearly and convincingly unique; shows originality and creativity • is free of wrong notes, flawed harmonies, or rhythmic errors • includes appropriate rehearsal marks • includes appropriate tempo markings • includes appropriate style markings • has form (not a form, but form) • is orchestrated/scored in accordance with conventions of quality that are specific to a particular genre, style, or performance medium (consider: melodic, harmonic, and rhythmic assignments; part assignments; textures; voicings) • is free of layout errors; is formatted in accordance with conventions of quality that are specific to the particular genre or style of music (consider: score order, stems, beaming, etc.) • uses keys that are congruent with the target audience • presents rhythmic challenges that are congruent with the target audience • presents a strategic balance of range demands that are congruent with the target audience • presents a strategic balance of technical demands that are congruent with the target audience • presents a strategic balance of endurance demands that are congruent with the target audience • presents a strategic balance of interpretive demands that are congruent with the target audience • [arranging only] is true to the original work; maintains the essence of the original work notate music with technology	music for specific purposes (e.g., to accompany, to enhance text). music that exemplifies specific genres or styles. music for specific performance mediums (vocal and/or instrumental). music for a variety of traditional and non-traditional sound sources. music for electronic instruments.
Destination	In contexts of diverse structure and sophistication, the students will be able to create music effectively and notate music proficiently. ⇕ *National Content Standards for Music, Grades K–12* (MENC, 1994) • Composing and arranging music within specified guidelines. • Notating music. ⇕ *National Standards for Arts Education* (Consortium of National Arts Education Associations, 1994, Introduction, § 4, ¶ 7) • [Students] should be able to communicate at a basic level in the four arts disciplines—dance, music, theatre, and the visual arts. This includes knowledge and skills in the use of the basic vocabularies, materials, tools, techniques, and intellectual methods of each arts discipline.	

60

Responding to Music

Pathway	[see Appendix A, Tables 6, 7, 8, 9a, and 9b] *The student is able to...*	when *responding to...*
	construct accurate analyses and descriptions, coherent evaluations, and meaningful connections	exemplary musical content and performances from various genres, styles, cultures, and historical periods.
Destination	In contexts of diverse structure and sophistication, the students will be able to analyze and describe music accurately, evaluate music and music performances coherently, and relate music meaningfully. ⇕ *National Content Standards for Music, Grades K–12* (MENC, 1994) • Listening to, analyzing, and describing music. • Evaluating music and music performances. • Understanding relationships between music, the other arts, and disciplines outside the arts. • Understanding music in relation to history and culture. ⇕ *National Standards for Arts Education* (Consortium of National Arts Education Associations, 1994, Introduction, § 4, ¶ 7) • [Students] should be able to develop and present basic analyses of works of art from structural, historical, and cultural perspectives, and from combinations of those perspectives. This includes the ability to understand and evaluate work in the various arts disciplines. • [Students] should have an informed acquaintance with exemplary works of art from a variety of cultures and historical periods, and a basic understanding of historical development in the arts disciplines, across the arts as a whole, and within cultures. • [Students] should be able to relate various types of arts knowledge and skills within and across the arts disciplines. This includes mixing and matching competencies and understandings in art-making, history and culture, and analysis in any arts-related project.

61

V

ARCHITECTURE STARTS WHEN YOU CAREFULLY PUT TWO BRICKS

TOGETHER.

THERE IT BEGINS.

—LUDWIG MIES VAN DER ROHE

According to John William Gardner, former Secretary of Health, Education, and Welfare, "All too often we are giving young people cut flowers when we should be teaching them to grow their own plants." Roger Lewin, noted author and anthropologist, agrees: "Too often we give our children answers to remember rather than problems to solve." Both perspectives capture the reality that learning is driven by action. As Einstein (1954) asserts, "The most important method of education...always has consisted of that in which the pupil was urged to actual participation" (p. 60). Consequently, *learning is revealed through performance* (Wiggins and McTighe, 1998, 2006), or through the execution of an action.

True or False?

We can't see inside students' brains. Teachers can only make inferences about learning by what students are able to do. (Kizlik, 2009)

In respect to building consequential units of study, these parallel principles—*learning is driven by action; learning is revealed through performance*—establish the foundation for a method of design that is as efficient as it is effective. This method revolves around four distinct yet interrelated processes that form a memorable acronym. The keyword is ***CARE.***

C ⇨ *Concentration*

A ⇨ *Accommodation*

R ⇨ *Reflection*

E ⇨ *Evaluation*

Concentration

⇕

Focus

Concentration is the process of establishing the objective(s) that will **63** *focus* a unit. To this end, teachers must do nothing less than the same—think objectively.

> The purpose of objectives is not to restrict spontaneity or constrain
> the vision of education in the discipline; but to ensure that learning is
> focused clearly enough that both students and teacher know what is
> going on, and so learning can be objectively *measured.* (Bixler, 2006,
> § 2, emphasis added)

Although there are many ways to specify an objective, a modified version of the classic "ABCD" model for writing "behavioral objectives" (Heinich, Molenda, Russell, and Smaldino, 1996) rises to the call. Distinctive to this model:

A represents Audience

B represents Behavior

C represents Condition

D represents Degree (of accuracy or mastery)

In the model presented on the pages that follow, A and B represent Authentic Behavior, while C and D represent Comprehensive Description of Quality (or Comprehensive Distinction).

SOMETIMES YOU NEED TO TAKE THE TIME

TO FIND TREASURES AND MOUNTAINS WE CAN CLIMB

AND MAYBE WE DREAM TO CHANGE THE WAY THAT WE FEEL

'CAUSE TO DREAMERS THE REAL WORLD CAN BE UNREAL

SARAH BRIGHTMAN • "DREAMERS"

AB ⇨ Authentic Behavior

To focus a unit of study, authenticity reigns supreme.

> Merriam-Webster's dictionary defines *authentic* as genuine and real…Brown, Collins, and Duguid (1989) described authentic activities as the "ordinary practices of the culture." According to Newmann and Wehlage (1993), authentic activities are real-world tasks that a person can expect to encounter on the job, in the home, or in other social contexts. (Woo, Herrington, Agostinho & Reeves, 2007, pp. 36–37)

According to McTighe and Wiggins (1999), asking students to "do" the subject is a means of assessing "the ability to efficiently and effectively use a repertoire of knowledge and skills to negotiate a complex task" (p. 140). Rich in educational value, authentic undertakings naturally create opportunities for students to practice, consult resources, and obtain feedback to revise and refine their work (Wiggins, 1998).

Like all core subject areas, music offers a host of opportunities for authentic engagement. Independently and in multiple combinations, the following behaviors offer infinite possibilities for designing real-world action:

- Analyzing music
- Arranging music
- Auditioning
- Collecting music
- Composing music and/or lyrics
- Conducting music
- Creating music videos
- Describing music, musicians, and music performances
- Evaluating music, musicians, and music performances
- Editing music
- Improvising
- Moving to music
- Organizing music

- Performing music (singing and playing instruments)
- Producing music
- Promoting music
- Recording music
- Selling music
- Sharing music
- Teaching music
- Transcribing music
- Using music-related technology

Example: Authentic, unit-level action (AB)

- At the spring concert and the Cherry Blossom Festival, the students will perform "America the Beautiful," "The Battle Hymn of the Republic," and "God Bless America."
- Using music notation software, the students will arrange "Shenandoah" for string quartet.
- The students will create album notes for a playlist of American masterworks.

Authenticity, which is not equal to complexity, is relevant to all grade levels and all types of music classes. Even the youngest students can engage in variations of three momentous themes: (1) performing music (e.g., singing), (2) creating music (e.g., improvising short musical answers on classroom instruments), and (3) responding to music (e.g., constructing simple yet accurate analyses and descriptions or playing singing games from world cultures).

True or False?
Authenticity connects learning to living.

CD ⇨ Comprehensive Description of Quality
Capacity without quality contradicts educational aims with lasting value and consequence. By referencing expectations for quality, the unit is grounded in

excellence. As a result, the guiding destination becomes twofold; it not only describes something to do, but also something done.

True to the dual meaning of "comprehensive," descriptions of quality can be broad and wide-ranging or more detailed and specific.

66

Example: Performing music

AB + CD   In live performance at the spring concert and the Cherry Blossom Festival, the students will perform "America the Beautiful," "The Battle Hymn of the Republic," and "God Bless America" with superior artistry.

⇕

AB   performing music

CD   superior artistry

Example: Creating music

AB + CD   Using music notation software, the students will create a grade two arrangement of "Shenandoah" that is rich in detail and correctly formatted for string quartet.

⇕

AB   using music notation software, arranging music

CD   grade two, rich in detail, correctly formatted

Example: Responding to music

AB + CD   Using appropriate terminology, the students will create comprehensive and critical album notes for a playlist of American masterworks.

⇕

AB   creating album notes

CD   using appropriate terminology, comprehensive and critical

True or False?

Without reference to quality, an objective is actually a "subjective."

It is important to note that AB + CD is a specific formula, not a specific form. An authentic musical behavior of particular quality can be expressed in many ways. Due to its very nature, authenticity also naturally aligns with one or more dimensions of musicianship.

Example: Variations of the AB + CD formula

Performing (+ Reading)

- In live performance at [event], the students will perform [titles] with superior artistry.
- In live performance at [event or location], the students will perform [titles of Christmas carols] with superior artistry.
- While marching in time, in style, and in form, the students will be able to perform [titles] with superior artistry.
- At the specified tempos, the students will perform a series of graded etudes and exercises with accuracy and expression.
- The students will perform [title of solo] with superior artistry.
- Within a Medieval banquet setting, the students will perform [titles] with superior artistry.
- In live performance at the "parents-only recital," the students will perform [titles] with characteristic tone quality and accuracy at the specified tempos.
- At sight, the students will perform [title] with accuracy and expression at the specified tempo(s).

Performing (+ Reading), Creating

- In live performance at [event], the students will perform [jazz titles] and improvise with superior artistry.
- The students will record an artistic album of [music that represents a select culture, genre, style, or historical period].

Performing, Creating, Evaluating

- In a drum circle, the students will improvise creatively and expressively.

- You are a blues musicians in the American South in the early part of the twentieth century. Create a blues song by writing an original lyric and improvising a melody to the lyrics. Your lyrics must be a minimum of 3 verses and follow the basic A–A1–B rhyme scheme. Your melody must fit the 12-bar blues form. Perform your song for your fellow "bluesicians" during an in-class jam session. Your classmates will decide who had the most creative and original performance. (West Virginia Department of Education, n.d., Teach 21 Instructional Guides: Choral Music, Advanced, Level III, Grades 8–12)

Performing (+ Reading), Analyzing and Describing, Evaluating

- The students will conduct an artistic performance of [title].

Creating (+ Notating), Relating

- The students will set a [poem or story] to music; the students will create music that accompanies a [poem or story].
- Using a portable keyboard (with headphones), the students will compose [original music within specific guidelines] that conveys a select mood, emotion, or sentiment.
- Using [name of music notation software], the students will compose music in treble and bass clefs to accompany and enhance [text, readings, dramatizations].

Creating (+ Notating)

- Using [name of music notation software] and [title of poem] for text, the students will create an artistic four-part *a cappella* composition.
- Using [name of music notation software], the students will create an artistic arrangement of [title that represents a select genre or style].
- Using [name of music notation software], the students will create an artistic arrangement of [title] for [specific medium].

- Using [name of music notation software], the students will compose [a "Sousa-style" march] for [brass quintet].
- Using [name of music notation software], the students will create a memorable "jingle" for [school activity, fundraising promotion, local non-profit organization, etc.].

69

Analyzing and Describing
- The students will construct an accurate and detailed analysis of [score].

Analyzing and Describing, Relating
- The students will create a comprehensive biography of [composer or artist].
- The students will create [analytic, descriptive, comprehensive] album notes for [playlist, recording].
- The students will create [analytic, descriptive, comprehensive] program notes for [concert, event].
- In groups of two and using [name of software], the students will construct a 10-minute audio-visual presentation that accurately describes the distinguishing characteristics and role of music in [specific culture or sub-culture].
- In groups of two and using [name of software], the students will construct an audio-visual presentation that accurately describes the evolution of [specific genre of American music].
- Using [name of software], the students will create an accurate audio-visual timeline of American patriotic songs and parallel historic events.
- The students will record a [30-minute] radio program that showcases the music of a [specific genre, style, artist, culture, or historical period].
- In groups of two, the students will create a 5-minute audio-visual presentation that accurately describes the characteristics, uses, and traditions of music in the Aboriginal culture.

Analyzing and Describing, Evaluating, Relating

- You and a partner are working to plan an international festival of music and dance in your town. As a rhythm and movement expert, you must listen to 3 recordings of different groups representing the same culture that would like to perform at your festival. You will document each recording according to tempo, rhythmic elements, and instrumentation. Then you will determine which group represents the music of their culture in the most authentic way. You must contact all 3 groups with written explanation as to why they were chosen or declined to perform in your festival. (West Virginia Department of Education, n.d., Teach 21 Instructional Guides: General Music, Grades 6–8)

- You are the editor for *Grove's Dictionary of Music and Musicians*. Prepare a dictionary entry for a selection you are playing in band that incorporates folk music. The entry should include information about the original sources, how the composer chose this material, and how the composition differs from the original version. (West Virginia Department of Education, n.d., Teach 21 Instructional Guides: Band, Advanced, Level III, Grades 5–12)

Performing (+ Reading), Relating

- In live performance at [event], the students will perform "The Trail of Tears" with superior artistry.
  ⇕
- The students will create a vivid bio-poem of a Native American who was forced to walk the Trail of Tears.

Performing (+ Reading), Creating (+ Notating),
Analyzing and Describing, Evaluating, Relating

- In live performance at [event], the students will perform "West Side Story" with superior artistry.
  ⇕
- Based on a select rivalry (in light of Jets/Sharks), the students will use [name of notation software] to compose two correctly

notated melodies that capture the spirit of each "side."

⇕

- Based on a select topic associated with "West Side Story," the students will create comprehensive notes for the program.

71

As illustrated in the preceding examples, AB + CD is a versatile formula for establishing clear, measurable, unit-level focus. For students, through the work of one or more "highly qualified" teachers, the result of the AB + CD formula is a consequential unit-level objective: to demonstrate an authentic musical behavior at a particular level of quality. The result is also a unit-level objective for the teacher: to equip students to demonstrate an authentic musical behavior at a particular level of quality. In respect to clarify, a unit-level objective derived with the AB + CD formula is one and the same as a culminating task or project.

VIRTUE IS RELATIVE AT BEST

THERE'S NOTHING WORSE THAN A SUNSET

WHEN YOU'RE DRIVING DUE WEST

ANI DIFRANCO • "VIRTUE"

Students learn best when working to achieve meaningful goals (Glasser, 1993; Marzano, 1992; Marzano, 2007; Wiggins and McTighe 1998/2006). In units of study driven by authenticity and excellence, meaning takes center stage by design. The operative words are *by design*, which does not necessarily equal "what I've always done." Indeed, even the most prototypical activities must be scrutinized for their ultimate purpose.

True or False?

We may be busy, we may be efficient, but we will only be effective if we begin with the end in mind.

—STEPHEN R. COVEY

Accommodation
⇕
Strategy

The process of *Concentration* brings clarity to unit-level objectives— culminating or milestone tasks that evolve when authentic musical behaviors merge with excellence and diverse, exemplary, and developmentally appropriate content. In turn, **Accommodation** is the process of designing lesson-level or rehearsal-level tasks that prepare the learner for and/or advance the learner toward successful performance of the culminating tasks—strategic planning. The aim is a course of action that accommodates need in two distinct yet inseparable forms:

1. Contextual Need – What should the students *do* to achieve the unit-level objective(s)? What type of musical action and methodologies will *empower* students for successful performance? Of course, intelligent answers must be adapted to the end; empowering pathways must be defined by the destination.

> In teaching as in carpentry, the selection of tools depends on the task at hand and the materials one is working with. Books and lectures *can* be wonderfully efficient modes of transmitting new information for learning, exciting the imagination, and honing students' critical faculties—but one would choose other kinds of activities to elicit from students their preconceptions and level of understanding, or to help them see the power of using meta-cognitive strategies to monitor their learning. Hands-on experiments *can* be a powerful way to ground emergent knowledge, but they do not alone evoke the underlying conceptual understandings that aid generalization. (Donovan, Bransford, and Pellegrino, 1999, pp. 18–19)

2. Universal Need – What kind of learning is important to all learners, regardless of context? What type of cross-disciplinary outcomes and methodologies will *enrich* the unit?

In response to these considerations, the following wisdom supports the construction of empowering and enriching pathways. Independently and in endless combinations, these ideas epitomize the essence of *Accommodation*— action in response to need.

> There is no universal best teaching practice…If, instead, the point of departure is a core set of learning principles, then the selection of teaching strategies (mediated, of course, by subject matter, grade level, and desired outcome) can be purposeful. The many possibilities then become a rich set of opportunities from which a teacher constructs an instructional program rather than a chaos of competing alternatives. (Donovan, Bransford, and Pellegrino, 1999, p. 19)

a. Where the senses fail us, reason must step in.

—GALILEO

Strategic tasks must be clearly measurable. If not, there is no way to determine if learning is present, absent, or in progress. To this end, as well as to maintain an emphasis on quality, a slightly modified version of the formula used to design unit-level tasks serves exceedingly well:

$$AB \Rightarrow \textit{Assessable} \text{ Behavior}$$
$$+$$
$$CD \Rightarrow \text{Comprehensive Description of Quality}$$

As with the design of unit-level tasks, AB + CD is a formula, not a form. "Assessable behavior" plus "comprehensive description of quality" is a formula for designing strategic tasks that are measurable and qualitative in form. Structurally, a strategic task can be traditional or creative, general or specific, simple or complex, and may apply to a single class period or several. A strategic task may also need to be tackled in conjunction with other tasks. In reference to voice, "speaking to the learner" helps to make learning personal.

For students, through the work of one or more "highly qualified" teachers, the result of the AB + CD formula is an empowering and/or enriching lesson- or rehearsal-level objective: to complete a strategic task at a particular level of quality. The result is also a lesson- or rehearsal-level objective for the teacher: to equip students to complete a strategic task at a particular level of quality.

Sample Objectives Using AB + CD Formula

Unit-Level Objective (AB + CD)	**Concentration**	Culminating Task ⇕ Destination
	In live performance at the spring concert and Cherry Blossom Festival, the students will perform "America the Beautiful," "The Battle Hymn of the Republic," and "God Bless America" with superior artistry.	
Lesson- or Rehearsal-Level Objectives (AB + CD)	**Accommodation** *To achieve the unit-level objective the student will:*	Strategic Tasks ⇕ Pathways
	Arrive at each rehearsal and performance on time with all required materials; contribute positively (e.g., give your complete attention to the conductor, perform your very best, do not interrupt the learning process for others, mark your part as needed to reduce repeat mistakes, stop when the conductor stops, etc.).	
	Arrive at each sectional on time with all required materials; contribute positively.	
	Demonstrate artistic performance of specific, teacher-selected excerpts of the concert music.	
	Create a recording of your parts; listen to your recording several times and create a list of at least ten ways to improve your performance; use the list to refine your performance; create a second recording; turn in your list and recordings by the deadline(s).	
	Use the instructor-provided rubrics to evaluate "run through" recordings of the concert music.	
	Use your completed rubrics to post responses to instructor-provided questions on the classroom website.	

Random samples of AB + CD tasks (strategic action):

- Perform [measures] of [title] with accuracy and expression at the specified tempo(s).
- Perform [exercises in a method book] with accurate pitch and rhythm.
- Perform [measures or sections] of [solo] from memory.
- Sing [phrase, excerpt, etude, exercise, or part] with a head tone.
- With a partner, complete [lesson 5] in [*Jump Right In*] correctly.
- Improvise a [24-measure] solo [with these pitches; in the key of B-flat].
- Create a 10-track playlist of exemplary [music in a select genre or style]. Present and defend your choices to the class.
- Create a score that is formatted correctly for [vocal and/or instrumental medium].
- Create a playlist of masterworks that represent [genre, style, artist, culture, historical period].
- Using a score and recording to [title], create a blueprint that accurately describes [elements of music].
- Using a score and recording to [title], construct an accurate "timbre timeline."
- Using a Venn diagram, identify at least [three] similarities and differences between [title] and [title].
- In complete sentences, create a K–W–L (Know–Want to Know–Learned) chart about [topic].
- After listening to class recordings, construct a complete sentence from each of the following prompts:
    The performance was good because….
    We could make the performance better by….
- After listening to the peer-generated playlist, write a short evaluation that incorporates [terms].
- Answer each question correctly on a quiz about musical traditions in the [culture or sub-culture].
- Using a class-generated scoring guide, write a 1-page evaluation of [*Sugarland's*] performance at the [Country Music Awards].

- List at least five similarities and differences between the roles and functions of [music in early America] and the roles and functions of [music in America today].
- With a partner, create a detailed mind-map of [topic].

76

    b. Standards serve as a frame of reference for judging the quality of practice. (Glasgow and Hicks, 2009)

True to the definition of "strategic action," achievement standards (e.g., GLEs and CLEs) are a means as well as an end.

Strategic Action ⇔ Using Achievement Standards to Design Lesson- or Rehearsal-Level Tasks

Concentration
In groups of [three] and based on a select *Grammy* category, the students will create a comprehensive [audio, audio-visual, oral] presentation for visitors at the Grammy Museum. – or – In groups of [two] and based on a select *Grammy* category, the students will create an educational brochure for visitors at the Grammy Museum.

Accommodation	Recurrent benchmarks in state and national achievement standards (core skills)	Reference *(see Appendix A)*
Using a graphic organizer, identify at least 5 similarities and differences between [year] *Grammy* winners in your category.	analyzing, classifying, comparing, contrasting, describing, expressing, or identifying music representing various genres and/or styles	Table 6
Create a crossword puzzle about your *Grammy* category. Be sure to incorporate each musical term on the teacher-provided list.	using musical terms	Table 6
Based on 2 *Grammy*-winning songs in your category, create a T-chart that accurately describes each element of music on the teacher-provided list.	analyzing, comparing, describing, discussing, explaining, or identifying elements of music	Table 6
Nominate a song or artist for a *Grammy* award in your category. Defend your nomination by explaining at least 3 specific reasons for your selection.	discussing, distinguishing, explaining, expressing, or knowing personal preferences for music	Table 7
Use the teacher-provided rubric to assess *Grammy*-nominated songs in your category from 2 different decades. Use your completed rubric to write a [1-page] comparative evaluation that is free of spelling and grammatical errors.	evaluating music or music performances by applying specific criteria	Table 7
Create a chart that describes at least [5] similarities and differences between *Grammy* winners in your category and *Grammy* winners in a foreign category.	analyzing, citing, comparing, describing, explaining, or identifying connections among arts	Table 8

c. Data data everywhere but not a thought to think.

—Theodore Roszak

Strategic action should always encompass "higher order" cognitive processing (i.e., analyzing, evaluating, and creating). Of course, a complete course of action will naturally encompass a variety of cognitive demands. As Lorin Anderson (2005), a former student of Benjamin Bloom, contends, analyzing, evaluating, and creating is often dependent upon, or "based on," remembering, understanding, and applying knowledge in factual, conceptual, or procedural form. For example, as part of a unit focused on music of the Romantic period, Mr. Elkins requires his students to identify titles and composers of masterworks from aural examples. As part of a unit focused on describing music, students in Ms. Amber's classroom work to correctly identify long-short, high–low, loud–soft, and fast–slow sounds.

d.

Knowledge comes, but wisdom lingers.
—Lord Tennyson

Common sense is not common.
—Will Rogers

Great minds ask great questions.
—Michael Gelb

Pearls of wisdom often appear in simple form, especially five-word phrases. In terms of designing empowering action for students to undertake, perhaps the most potent five-word phrase of all-time is offered by cognitive scientist Daniel T. Willingham (2004): *"Memory is as thinking does"* (p. 75). This quintet of wisdom—students will only remember what they think about—applies to both the focus and the extent of thinking.

Strategic action ⇔ *"Memory is as thinking does."*

Which of the following tasks
are more likely to provoke focused thinking?

Submitting a practice card (with a signature that was likely forged).	*or*	Creating a self-recording.
Watching a video.	*or*	Watching a video to answer specific questions; watching a video in short segments so students can "retell the story."
Reading a chapter.	*or*	Reading a chapter to answer an extensive list of multiple-choice questions.
Visiting select websites.	*or*	Visiting select websites and writing a short review.
Listening to a lecture and taking notes.	*or*	1. Using teacher-provided resources in small groups to find answers to specific questions.
		2. Reviewing answers with the teacher, as a class, and in groups.
		3. Applying the information, individually or in groups, to complete a summarizing task.
Writing an assignment in a notebook.	*or*	Writing down an assignment and then explaining it to a partner/peer.
Taking notes.	*or*	Using notes to write a summary of the day's lesson.

(adapted from Rosenshine, 1997)

e.

BLIND MELON • "THREE IS A MAGIC NUMBER"

At all levels of musical complexity, a superior performance is captivating—the music and the musicians connect with (speak to) the audience. Inherent to such a performance is a multiplicity of parts that come together to create a moving whole, courtesy of craftsmen, artists, and enlightened thinkers all wrapped into one.

Music performers are craftsman in the sense that they recreate or construct musical notation—elements that are *built* into music by the composer or arranger. Music performers are artists in the sense that each performance is stamped with the music-makers' unique musical personality and interpretation. Elements such as tone quality, intonation, dynamic nuances, and tempo fluctuations are *brought* to music by the musician and contribute to the overall expressiveness, character, and impact of the performance.

DON'T PLAY WHAT'S THERE, PLAY WHAT'S NOT THERE.
—MILES DAVIS

Have you ever heard a superior performance that did not reflect great craft and art? Likely not. These elements are key players in such a performance, but they are not alone.

So Monet was painting at the same time that Debussy and Ravel were composing. While these great masters were influencing each other in the creation of works of art, we were in the middle of World War I, and the first solo non-stop transatlantic air flight was about to take off from Long Island. Why didn't anyone ever teach me these things? (Miceli, 2003, p. 22)

This reflection by professor Jennifer Scott Miceli illuminates a third factor related to superior performance. It also reveals the prevalence of its absence, which is unfortunate. Uncovering connections to significant people, places, things, and events that dwell *behind* the music—making interdisciplinary connections—is actually a means of enhancing performance, e.g., "the knowledge that Haydn and Mozart lived at approximately the same time helps the learner conceptualize style" (Boardman, 2001, p. 49). As Cosenza (2005) argues,

Music teachers may think they are losing instructional time in the service of other subjects when, in fact, if music teachers understand the cognitive connections and shared information among subjects, they have opportunities to enhance music learning in substantive and authentic ways. *(abstract)*

The moral of this story extends far beyond music performance and crosses borders throughout the field. For all types of music classes, the "built-brought-behind" trio is a triple play: a strategy for designing curricula, enhancing achievement, and respecting the overarching directive of standards—comprehensive music education.

STRATEGY WITHOUT TACTICS IS THE SLOWEST ROUTE TO VICTORY.

TACTICS WITHOUT STRATEGY IS THE NOISE BEFORE DEFEAT.

—SUN TZU

⇩

82

Built: What can students *do* to demonstrate understanding of essential elements related to the music, topic, or theme?

Brought: What can students *do* to demonstrate understanding of artistry related to the music, topic, or theme?

Behind: What can students *do* to demonstrate understanding of important or meaningful facts and concepts related to the music, topic, or theme?

Strategic Action ⇔ *The "Built–Brought–Behind Strategy"*

Grade Level: Secondary **Course: General Music**	
Accommodation ⇕ *Pathway*	Create a "blueprint" for [title of representative masterwork] that accurately describes the following elements: pitch, rhythm, harmony, dynamics, timbre, texture, and form. Construct a "3-D listening guide" for [select music genre] by providing comprehensive answers to the following questions: *Side 1* (Explanation, Analysis, Description) What are some exemplary examples of this music? What are the defining characteristics of this music? *Side 2* (Application) Where is this music likely to be heard? How could this music be used? *Side 3* (Empathy) Why do people create this music? *Side 4* (Perspective) What is unique about this music? What do other people have to say about this music? *Side 5* (Evaluation) Why do I like or dislike this music? What titles would make up my top 10 playlist? *Side 6* (Self-Knowledge) What are my "blind spots" about this music? What are the influences on my opinion about this music? (adapted from the "Six Facets of Understanding," Wiggins and McTighe, 1998/2006) Use your blueprint, 3-D project, and the teacher-provided guidelines to create your poster.
Concentration ⇕ *Destination*	For use in elementary music classrooms, the students will construct a scaled model of an informational poster that accurately and creatively describes [select music genre].
	analyzing and describing, evaluating, relating

Grade Level: Secondary **Course: Choral or Instrumental Ensemble**		
Accommodation ⇕ **Pathway**	1	2
	Arrive at each rehearsal and performance on time with all required materials; contribute positively.	Select a topic associated with the concert music from the teacher-provided list. Create at least 5 open-ended questions about your topic. Turn in your questions for approval.
	Arrive at each sectional on time with all required materials; contribute positively.	
	Demonstrate artistic performance of specific, instructor-selected excerpts of the concert music.	Locate at least 3 sources from the library and 3 sources from the Internet that provide answers to your questions.
	Create a recording of your parts; listen to your recording several times and create a list of at least 10 ways to improve your performance; use the list to refine your performance; create a second recording; turn in your list and recordings by the deadline(s)	Create a first draft by (a) combining information from your sources to answer each of your questions, (b) sequencing your answers to tell an interesting story, and (c) citing your sources correctly.
	Use the instructor-provided rubrics to evaluate "run through" recordings of the concert music. Use your completed rubrics to post responses to instructor-provided questions on the classroom website.	Ask 2 adults to proofread and sign your work. Use the feedback and teacher-provided rubric to revise your work. Turn in your original and revised drafts by the deadline. Use your final draft to create a 1-minute presentation that summarizes important discoveries from your investigation. Give your presentation to the class on the assigned date.
Concentration ⇕ **Destination**	In live performance at the spring concert and Cherry Blossom Festival, the students will perform "America the Beautiful," "The Battle Hymn of the Republic," and "God Bless America" with superior artistry	Based on a select topic associated with the concert music, the students will create comprehensive notes for the program.
	performing, reading, evaluating	analyzing and describing, relating

True or False?

This unit is focused on that which is built into the music, brought to the music, and behind the music.

True or False?

This unit consists entirely of measurable activities that equip students to successfully achieve the unit-level objectives.

True or False?

This unit demands exemplary music;
its power comes from the work of exceptional musicians.

True or False?

The "teacher-provided" topics, rubric, and practice assignments in this unit could be modified or enhanced to meet diverse learner needs.

True or False?

Many students could record, listen to, and e-mail excerpts of practice material with a smart phone…which could also be used as a metronome and tuner.

True or False?

Technology has forever changed the experience of music (Kratus, 2007).

True or False?

This unit focuses on "problems to solve" rather than "answers to remember."

True or False?

This unit is "off the chart" in terms of higher-order thinking.

True or False?

This unit could be adapted to multiple grade levels.

True or False?

This is a departure from the status-quo…but I could do this.

f. There is no I in team…but there is in win.

—MICHAEL JORDAN

To win in unit design, to construct a firm foundation for meaningful lesson planning and instruction, serious consideration must be given to the individual. Specifically, how can the teacher infer that each learner has learned? This is particularly relevant to performance-based music classrooms (e.g., bands, orchestras, and choirs).

g. There is no greater impediment to the advancement of knowledge than the ambiguity of words.

—THOMAS REID

What terminology/vocabulary is central to successful performance? Just imagine the constructive outcomes that could result if every student perceived key terms in the same manner. After all, "teaching" is a verb, right?

h. Where all think alike, no one thinks very much.

—WALTER LIPPMANN

To accommodate variations in learning styles, as well as the nature and variety of "human intellectual competences (Gardner, 1983, p. 31)—students should be allowed to demonstrate learning in various ways. For example:

Visual	Performance	Written	Oral	Multimedia
Cartoon/Comic	Dance	Short Story/Book	Debate	PowerPoint Slide Show
Collage	Monologue	Magazine	Discussion	Game/Game Show
Diorama	Play/Musical	Essay/Report	Talk Show	TV Show/Movie
Mobile	Simulation	Song/Rap/Poem	Interview	Website
Sculpture	Experiment	Newsletter/Newspaper	Speech	Exhibit

(District of Columbia Public Schools, 2008–09, p. 42)

i. The illiterate of the 21st century will not be those who cannot read and write, but those who cannot learn, unlearn, and re-learn.

—ALVIN TOFFLER

Incorporating opportunities to integrate, extend, and refine core 21st century skills—developing and demonstrating multiple literacy—is applicable to virtually all descriptions of quality unit design.

j. I am a citizen, not of Athens or Greece, but of the world.

—SOCRATES

Activities that help students to see the world through the eyes of others honors the fact that *diversity is the one true thing we all have in common.* Examples include service projects, activities that engage parents and community members, and tasks that illuminate connections with people from diverse cultures, past and present.

k. Time is a Judge. Things that stand the test of time pass the greatest test.

—UNKNOWN

Activities and sequences of activities aligned with the philosophies and pedagogies of Edwin Gordon, Emile Jaques-Dalcroze, Zoltan Kodály, and Carl Orff are more than deserving of serious consideration.

l. We are what we repeatedly do. Excellence then, is not an act, but a habit.

—ARISTOTLE

For those who have taught for even a day, the concept of "revision" requires little justification. Guidance in the realm of refinement is important for all but the most conscientious learners. The name of the game is quality control; the aim is to clearly illuminate something of immense value: the paths to improvement. Without frequent opportunities to revise and refine their work, students may perceive doing, in and of itself, as the target. This, however, is only half the equation, as capacity without quality is bleak in ultimate value.

Although pathways to improvement can come in many forms, five are particularly effective. Independently or in combination, these dynamic mediums for revision and refinement can help students to perform at their best.

- *Exemplars* – Compare work to exceptional examples ("Oh, so this is what you want").
- *Self-recordings* – Use an aural picture to revise and refine performance.
- *Rubrics* – Compare work to teacher-constructed, class-constructed, or self-constructed scoring guides or performance scales.
- *Self-assessment checklists* – Connect effort to outcome.
- *Reflections* – Learning requires reflection as well as experience. Through systematic reflective tasks or journal entries students may see the value of persistence and effort, which supports the motivating mindset: "I am capable of accomplishing great things." On the other hand, they may identify errors or shortcomings, which is the first step toward improvement.

Strategic Action ⇔
Connecting Effort to Outcome with a Self-Assessment Checklist

Concentration
performing, reading
In live performance at the spring concert and Cherry Blossom Festival, the students will perform "America the Beautiful," "The Battle Hymn of the Republic," and "God Bless America" with superior artistry.

Accommodation	
Complete the self-assessment checklist.	❑ I arrived at each rehearsal on time with instrument, music, and pencil.
Arrive at each rehearsal and performance on time with all required materials; contribute positively.	❑ I arrived at each sectional on time with instrument, music, and pencil. ❑ I contributed positively to each sectional and rehearsal by:
Arrive at each sectional on time with all required materials; contribute positively.	❑ practicing my parts as assigned ❑ arriving prepared ❑ participating fully ❑ demonstrating proper rehearsal etiquette.
Complete specific practice assignments designated by the conductor.	❑ I recorded my parts. ❑ I used my recording to create a list of at least 10 ways to improve my performance.
Create a recording of your parts; listen to your recording several times and create a list of at least 10 ways to improve your performance; use the list to refine your performance; create a second recording; turn in your list and recordings by the deadline(s).	❑ I used my list to refine my performance; I practiced everything on my list. ❑ I made a second recording. ❑ I turned in my list and recordings by the deadline.
Use the instructor-provided rubrics to evaluate "run-through" recordings of the concert music.	❑ I used the instructor-provided rubrics to evaluate "run-through" recordings of the concert music.
Use your completed rubrics to post responses to instructor-provided questions on the classroom website.	❑ I used my completed rubrics to post comments on the classroom website. ❑ I was dressed properly and ready to go at call times.

Strategic Action ⇔ *Encouraging Revision and Refinement*

Accommodation	Concentration
❑ At least [#] weeks before the audition, create a self-recording.	AB + CD: At a live audition on [date], the students will perform the All-District Honor Choir etudes with superior artistry.
❑ Ask the instructor and at least one other musician to evaluate your recording.	
❑ Use the feedback and the instructor-provided rubric to refine your performance and create a second self-recording.	
❑ Ask the instructor and at least one other musician, someone different than the first time, to evaluate your recording.	
❑ Attend the pre-audition recital.	
❑ Attend the mock audition.	
❑ Arrive at the audition site, in proper attire, at least one hour before your audition time.	
Pathway	**Destination**

> nobody wants to see it
>
> they don't even wanna try
>
> judge a book by its cover and you'll never know the story
>
> there's so much more than meets the eye
>
> CELINE DION • "EVERYBODY'S TALKIN' MY BABY DOWN"
> SONGWRITERS: RUSSELL DE SALVO, ARNOLD ROMAN

By specifying student-centered action that is focused, measurable, empowering, and enriching, something wonderful and powerful is born: the basis for meaningful *assessment, feedback,* and *evaluation.*

To avoid misinterpretation of these common terms, a point of clarification is in order (monumental understatement). "Assessment" is a noun—as in objective or subjective measurement or examination of learner performance through one or more of the senses. "Assess" is a verb—as in to measure or examine learner performance through one or more of the senses. Thus, in everyday use, the term "assessment" often refers to an "opportunity to assess" or a "means of assessing." In relation to objective or subjective standards of quality, "feedback" and "evaluation" are verbal, non-verbal, formal, or informal responses (end) derived from assessment/assessing (means). For example:

Assessment:	Watching a student shoot free throws; counting the number of free throws the student successfully shoots.
Feedback/Evaluation:	"You made 4 out of 28 free throws…which stinks." (Duke, 2005, p. 53)

Assessment:	Listening to (and watching) a student sing.
Feedback/Evaluation:	"Your performance was exceptional. You sang with beautiful tone quality and expressiveness."

Assessment:	Grading a quiz; comparing student responses to correct responses.
Feedback/Evaluation:	"All questions were answered correctly; you earned an A."

In context, a culminating task (Concentration) is a means of summative assessment. Each strategic task that follows (Accommodation) is a means of formative assessment.

> When we speak of evidence of [learning], we are referring to evidence gathered through a variety of formal and informal assessments during a unit of study or course. We are not alluding only to end-of-teaching tests or culminating performance tasks. Rather, the collected evidence we seek may include observations and dialogues, traditional quizzes and tests, performance tasks and projects, as well as students' self-assessments gathered over time. (Wiggins and McTighe, 2006, p. 169)

At both the unit and program levels, the potential impact of frequent assessment is something to revere. Every performance by a learner is a spark for meaningful feedback, modifications, or enhancements; frequent assessment provides the information that teachers need to keep students moving forward (Schmoker, 1999).

92

> Formative assessments—ongoing assessments designed to make students' thinking visible to both teachers and students—are essential. They permit the teacher to grasp the students' preconceptions, understand where the students are in the "developmental corridor" from informal to formal thinking, and design instruction accordingly. In the assessment-centered classroom environment, formative assessments help both teachers and students monitor progress. (Donovan, Bransford, and Pellegrino, 1999, p. 21)

True or False?

Most students don't do what's expected, only what's inspected.

Systematic assessment is also important due to its relationship with metacognition, or "thinking about thinking," knowing "what we know," and "what we don't know" (Blakely and Spence, 1990, ¶ 1). According to Donovan, Bransford, and Pellegrino (1999), the integration of metacognitive activities can "enhance student achievement and develop in students the ability to learn independently" (p. 17). Through frequent assessment, students' thinking becomes "visible to themselves, their peers, and their teacher," which "provides feedback that can guide modification and refinement in thinking" (p. 15).

True or False?

"Assessment" is a synonym for Accommodation.

R.   *Reflection*
⇕

re·flec·tion
n a clear indication or result of something
(*reflection*, def. 1)

In a consequential program of study, a unit of study must clearly provide convincing *evidence* (E) of emerging musicianship. When this is not the case, when achievement does not represent learning that is of central or fundamental importance to the learner, the unit is effectively "cluttering the curriculum" (Bruner, 1960). Thus, the process of Reflection aims at identifying or referencing the local priorities that are revealed when students successfully achieve an objective. "Local priorities," which will naturally encompass multiple contextual and universal needs, could range from state and national standards to data-derived instructional strategies to a host of "current" grade-level, program-level, building-level, or district-level agendas.

Simple Reflection

	Grade Level: Secondary Title: Read All About It	
Concentration	For use in elementary music classrooms, the students will construct a scaled model of an informational poster that accurately and creatively describes [select musical genre].	
Accommodation	Construct a "3-D listening guide" for [select musical genre] by providing comprehensive answers to the following questions: Side 1 (Explanation, Analysis, Description) What are some exemplary examples of this music? What are the defining characteristics of this music? Side 2 (Application) Where is this music likely to be heard? How could this music be used? Side 3 (Empathy) Why do people create this music? Side 4 (Perspective) What is unique about this music? What do other people have to say about this music? Side 5 (Evaluation) Why do I like or dislike this music? What titles would make up my top 10 playlist? Side 6 (Self-Knowledge) What are my "blind spots" about this music? What are the influences on my opinion about this music?	*Grade-Level Standards, e.g.,* 7.6.1 Identify and describe musical elements such as rhythmic and melodic ideas, tonality, form, expressive qualities, and timbre through discussion, writing, or illustration, including how these elements might convey a particular emotion or mood. 7.6.3 Identify and use appropriate terminology to describe various musical styles, genres, cultures, and time periods. 7.7.1 Define and discuss characteristics of a variety of effective musical works such as repetition and contrast and rhythmic and melodic interest. 7.7.2 Listen to and compare examples of a particular style or genre using basic music terminology. 7.8.5 Identify music related to a contemporary event or topic and explore interdisciplinary connections that involve music performance, dramatization, related art, reading, writing, and other potential activities. 7.9.4 Explore various musical styles and genres from Asia, Africa, Europe, and the Americas. 7.9.5 Respond to specific writing prompts such as, "Is music valued in our culture, how, and by whom?"	**Reflection** (Indiana Department of Education, 2007)
	Create a "blueprint" for [title of representative masterwork] that accurately describes the following elements: pitch, rhythm, harmony, dynamics, timbre, texture, and form.	
	Use your blueprint, 3-D project, and the teacher-provided guidelines to create your poster.	
	AB + CD	***= E***

Simple Reflection

	Grade Level: Secondary **Title: Whoo! Whoo!**		
Concentration	In live performance at the heritage assembly, the students will perform *"I've Been Workin' on the Railroad," "John Henry,"* and *"Casey Jones"* accurately, expressively, and from memory.		
Accommodation (adapted from Bolar, 2004)	Demonstrate your best rehearsal behavior at every class meeting. With your partners, sing teacher-selected phrases accurately, expressively, and from memory.	*Grade-Level Standards*, e.g., P1A1: Use a singing voice with a head tone PP1A2: Demonstrate appropriate singing posture PP1A2: Apply accurate pitch relationships while singing in a limited range PP1B2, PP2B2: Demonstrate loud and soft dynamics and fast and slow tempos PP1C2: Perform a varied repertoire of songs, including patriotic, folk, seasonal, and spirituals PP1E2, PP2E2: Perform in groups using a steady beat, matching dynamics, following the cues of the conductor HC1C2: Discuss and demonstrate appropriate listening behavior for various types of performances HC1D1: Identify responsibilities of a music leader and group participants in a classroom setting or performance ensemble setting	**Reflection** (Missouri Department of Elementary and Secondary Education, 2007)
	Using mini white boards, respond to the teacher's questions and instructions about unfamiliar words and symbols in the railroad songs.	IC1A1: Name words and ideas that are used to describe works of art EP1C2: Identify $\boldsymbol{p}$ for *piano* and $\boldsymbol{f}$ for *forte*	
	Identify at least three similarities and differences between the railroad songs (e.g., use a Venn Diagram, mind map, analogies, T-chart, right brain-left brain note pad, concept web, or concept map to identify similarities and differences between form, tempo, dynamics, stories, etc.).	AP1A2: Recognize basic forms and composition techniques, including question/answer, call/response, AB, repeated patterns (ostinati), verse/refrain, repeat sign, and introduction HC1A2: Identify characteristics of teacher-selected genres or styles HC1B2: Describe how elements of music are used in teacher-selected examples HC1C2: Describe the function of music in various settings and cultural events	
	Homework: From memory, sing each railroad song for a grown-up while they complete the teacher-provided checklist.	PP1A2: Demonstrate appropriate singing posture PP1B2, PP2B2: Demonstrate loud and soft dynamics and fast and slow tempos	

Accommodation (cont.)		Reflection (cont.)
With your partners, create a checklist for grading class recordings (audio-visual) of the railroad songs. Use your checklist to grade class recordings of the railroad songs.	AP2A2 Develop criteria to distinguish between quality and non-quality performance through listening and self-assessment with regard to the following musical elements: appropriate singing voice, loud/soft, steady beat, posture/stage presence	
After watching the video on western expansion, identify at least three similarities between railroad songs and western expansion.	IC1B2 Identify ways in which the principles and subject matter of other disciplines are interrelated with those of music	
Describe the tall tale in *"John Henry."* Create your own tall tale about the school mascot. Using a barred instrument, create music that accompanies ("sounds good with") your tall tale.	IC1B2 Identify ways in which the principles and subject matter of other disciplines are interrelated with those of music PP4A1 Create a single tone or non-pitched accompaniment for songs and stories	
Identify at least 3 similarities between *"Casey Jones"* and American heroes. Write three complete sentences that describe a personal hero; share with the class.	AP2B2 Use prerequisite music terms to describe their personal response to a musical example (feelings, images/stories, tempo) IC1B1 List common themes found in all subject areas (e.g., repetition) IC1B2 Identify ways in which the principles and subject matter of other disciplines are interrelated with those of music	
Create two questions about railroad songs to ask a classroom visitor—a real train conductor. Write a thank you note to the guest conductor; describe at least one thing that you learned.	HC1A2 Identify characteristics of teacher-selected genres or styles HC1C2 Describe the function of music in various settings and cultural events	
AB + CD	= E	

Comprehensive Reflection

Course: Grade Level: Title:			**Accommodation:** Lesson-Level or Rehearsal- Level Objectives				**Concentration:** Unit-Level Objective
Duration/Class Periods			I	2	3	⇨	
AB + CD							
Reflection: Alignment with Local Priorities	**= E**	Essential Questions					
		Enduring Understandings The student understands that…					
		Factual Knowledge The student knows…					
		National Content Standards					
		GLEs/CLEs: Music					
		GLEs/CLEs: Other Subjects					
		State Content Standards					
		State Process or "Power" Standards					
		21st Century Skills					
		Habits of Mind					
		Depth of Knowledge					
		Bloom's Taxonomy (Cognitive Processes)					
		Multiple Intelligences					
		Learning Styles					
		Character-Related Connections					
		Diversity-Related Connections					

See Appendix B for a complete example of comprehensive reflection.

97

True or False?

This type of Reflection could reveal curricular gaps or unnecessary redundancies within a series of units or an entire program of study.

vary dramatically. Deserving of special note, however, is making connections with overarching understandings that dwell at the core of the discipline—concepts that all musicians should come to understand. To this end, essential questions are doorways to understanding (Wiggins and McTighe, 2006); they help students construct meaning within a subject, think and perform like experts (i.e., musicians), and interact with concepts that are "alive" in a field of study (Wiggins, 2007). If not, are they really "essential"?

Answers to compelling questions can take many forms. Students can speak answers, document answers, or demonstrate answers (e.g., "Sing it to me."). Thus, every successful performance throughout a unit of study is effectively an answer to a question. This is key to understanding the relationship between essential questions and skill-oriented curricula. When students do something well—something *essential*—they are also demonstrating an answer to a question of equal importance. Just ask.

Overarching Skills	*Overarching Understandings, e.g.,*	*Overarching Questions, e.g.,*
Performing music artistically	Developing a skill is a process: deliberately first; naturally second. A musical performance labeled "superior," "exceptional," or "artistic" meets or exceeds conventions of quality. Conventions of quality include both objective and subjective criteria. Conventions of quality vary among practices.	What kind of practice makes perfect? How does this go? What clear and hidden messages did the composer leave for me/us? How well can I perform this? What does it mean when a performance is labeled superior, exceptional, or artistic? How does change and consistency contribute to musical artistry?
Creating music effectively	Music enables you to "talk to" people who aren't there. Artists often break with established traditions, conventions, and techniques to express what they see and feel. Composers sometimes convey ideas indirectly. When words fail, music speaks. Art is only limited by the imagination.	What is a complete musical thought? How can you say something without saying it? How can I create [type of composition or arrangement]? How can I use [type of compositional technique] to organize my ideas?
Reading music proficiently	Music is a universal language.	Why keep reading?
Analyzing and describing music accurately	Music is composed of key elements—pitch, rhythm, harmony, dynamics, timbre, texture, and form (MENC, 1994, Glossary). Insightful analysis of music, in lieu of shallow criticism, requires listening for elements of music and how they conspire to form significant wholes. Music is organized sound.	What is this? Why is it important? What am I listening for? Who is this? Why is [name] important? In all of your favorite music, what never changes? How does form follow function?

100

Overarching Skills	Overarching Understandings, e.g.,	Overarching Questions, e.g.,
Evaluating music coherently	Beauty is in the eye of the educated beholder. Opinion and perspective are two different things.	Why do I like or dislike this? How is this unique? What's so special about this? How does the medium influence the message?
Relating music meaningfully	Art imitates life. Music shapes and is shaped by society and culture. Music is simultaneously personal and global.	How does art reflect as well as shape culture? How is art both a window and a mirror?

True or False?

An essential question is a doorway to understanding;
a performance is a demonstration of understanding.

True or False?

An infinite array of *strategic* questions is subsumed
in an overarching question.

In sum, and regardless of "what" is referenced, the process of **Reflection** asks the designer(s) of a unit to reflect—as in to give serious or careful thought to meaningful connections. Consequently, the unit will inevitably undergo revision and refinement to establish nothing less than the same—reflection. In other words, through the back-and-forth, give-and-take interaction of **Concentration**, **Accommodation**, and **Reflection**, a unit of study evolves through the incessant consideration of specific priorities. As a result, a thought can turn into a brilliant idea. A spark can grow into a brilliant flame. An assessment can become a powerful force for meaningful and accountable change.

IT IS NOT ENOUGH TO BE BUSY, SO ARE THE ANTS.
THE QUESTION IS, "WHAT ARE WE BUSY ABOUT?"
—HENRY DAVID THOREAU

IT'S NOT SO MUCH HOW BUSY YOU ARE, BUT WHY YOU ARE BUSY.   **101**
THE BEE IS PRAISED. THE MOSQUITO IS SWATTED.
—MARY O'CONNOR

 ## *Evaluation*
⇕

Illuminate hallmarks of quality.

The final process within the C-A-R-E formula is designing evaluative instrumentation that brings precise clarity to "comprehensive descriptions of quality." In support of this charge, perhaps no greater methodology exists than the construction of rubrics, which are also known as scoring guides and performance scales. Rubrics can be adapted to almost any type of performance and promote quality by providing criterion-referenced feedback. According to Marzano, Pickering, and Pollock (2001), "Criterion-referenced feedback is superior to norm-referenced feedback. In nontechnical terms, this means that providing students with feedback in terms of specific levels of knowledge and skill is better than simply providing students with a percentage score." (p. 99).

As revealed through the following examples, a well-crafted rubric not only defines quality, but also shows that such work is achievable (Schmoker, 1999).

1. Responding to Music

Sample Rubric for Assessing Written Responses to Music

The description/response:	SA	A	PA	D	SD
	5	4	3	2	I
clearly completes the assignment.					
conveys information clearly; the reader can easily grasp the writer's message; detail is appropriate.					
conveys information that is accurate, credible, plausible, or important.					
is presented in an orderly fashion; the sequence of information is not confusing.					
is insightful.					
is individual and powerful.					
is free of misspelled words.					
is free of grammatical errors.					
is neat in appearance/presentation/format.					
is a model for future students.					

SA = Strongly Agree   A = Agree
PA = Partially Agree   D = Disagree
SD = Strongly Disagree

2. Creating Music

Sample Score Scoring Scoreboard

Indicator	5	4	3	2	1
Accessibility	Range is within practical limits; strategic balance of demand	Range is within practical limits; demand is appropriate for target audience	Range is generally within practical limits; demand is inconsistent	Range is often outside of practical limits; demand is inconsistent and/or random	Range is often outside of practical limits; demand is extreme and/or random
Voicing	Instruments are voiced in accordance with standard conventions except when artistic freedom necessitates otherwise	Instruments are generally voiced in accordance with standard conventions	Inconsistent voicing in relation to standard conventions	Voicing is frequently inconsistent and/or unconventional	Voicing is inconsistent and/or unconventional throughout
Layout and Presentation	Score is exceptionally clean and uniform throughout; free of engraving errors	Score is predominately uniform; minimal engraving errors	Score is predominately uniform; frequent engraving errors	Uniformity of score is inconsistent; several engraving errors	Presentation of score is not uniform; conventions of engraving ignored
Creativity	Orchestration clearly and convincingly shows evidence of creative thought; stands alone	Orchestration shows frequent evidence of creative thought	Orchestration shows moderate evidence of creative thought	Orchestration shows minimal evidence of creative thought	Orchestration shows no evidence of creative thought
Attention to Detail	Score clearly and convincingly includes markings that will aid performers in achieving the desired performance result(s)	Score frequently includes markings that will aid performers in achieving the desired performance result(s)	Score occasionally includes markings that will aid performers in achieving the desired performance result(s)	Score seldom includes markings that will aid performers in achieving the desired performance result(s)	Score does not include markings that will aid performers in achieving the desired performance result(s)

3. Performing Music – Think back to the most perfectly "superior" performance you can remember, or a music-making experience that challenged your perception of the ideal. What dimensions of this performance captivated you most? What sounds and/or images are most vivid? What words could be used to capture the essence of such a performance? Perhaps these thoughts on perfect or "100 point" wines by James Suckling (2005) can provide some inspiration:

Like evaluating a lover, rating a wine has a deeply subjective component. Perfect wines have everything and even more; it's that wow-factor, that spellbinding quality that makes your jaw drop in amazement. Some might call it sex appeal. Others might say intrigue or simple chemistry. Whatever it is, I have always found some intangible quality that is nearly impossible to articulate. You just know that it's an extraordinary wine.

But there are some objective requirements. In general, fine wines must have structure and balance; perfect wines display this flawlessly…A perfect wine [also] must communicate something specific and exciting about its *terroir*, its growing season and its producer. These wines are unique expressions of a certain place at a certain time. They are like works of art that reflect the talent of the artist as well as the moment they were created. No two perfect wines can be identical. (p. 60)

Exceptional music performances are much the same. No two are identical, and musical artistry is definitely a complex blend of objective and subjective components that communicate something about its producer. In terms of teaching students to perform music artistically, however, the former is where the magic begins. As revealed through recurrent benchmarks of achievement in state and national standards (See Appendix A, Table 2), a dose of objectivity is the doorway to subjective understanding:

Achievement Standard		Publications	EL	MS	HS	Total	Generalizations
							The student is able to:
singing or playing	with appropriate posture	5	8	20	19	47	maintain appropriate body and/or instrument position.
singing or playing	with characteristic tone quality	4	12	17	15	44	perform with a clear and resonant tone, regardless of range or dynamic level.
	with proper breath support	5	3	20	13	36	
singing or playing	with accurate rhythm	5	11	16	11	38	perform pitches and rhythms accurately at the appropriate tempo(s).
	with a steady beat	5	18	2	12	32	
	accurately	4	4	5	10	19	
singing	with technical accuracy	5	7	23	24	54	[vocal performance] perform with appropriate diction; articulate text clearly and accurately.
playing	with technical accuracy	5	7	29	17	53	[instrumental performance] perform with proper and fluid instrumental technique.
singing or playing	with appropriate intonation	5	15	25	26	66	adjust tone quality/ timbre, intonation/pitch, and volume to blend with other voices or instruments; perform with accurate intervallic relationships.
	with appropriate blend	5	6	6	11	23	
	with appropriate balance	4	1	7	12	20	
singing or playing	with stylistic accuracy	3	2	9	3	14	perform with stylistic accuracy or as specified by the composer, arranger, or conductor.
	with sensitivity to performance practices	3	0	10	0	10	
singing or playing	expressively	5	11	34	21	66	vary and adjust timbre, motion, articulation, dynamics, and phrasing as needed or as specified by the composer, arranger, or conductor to construct an expressive performance.
	with appropriate dynamics	5	19	25	20	64	
	with appropriate phrasing	5	7	16	21	44	
	with appropriate interpretation	3	2	2	2	6	

Sample Rubric for Music Performance Derived from
Recurrent Benchmarks in State and National Achievement Standards

106

The student:	SA 5	A 4	PA 3	D 2	SD 1
maintains appropriate body and/or instrument position.					
performs with a clear and resonant tone, regardless of range or dynamic level.					
performs pitches and rhythms accurately at the appropriate tempo(s).					
[instrumental performance] performs with proper and fluid instrumental technique.					
[vocal performance] performs with appropriate diction; articulates text clearly and accurately.					
adjusts tone quality/timbre, intonation/pitch, and volume to blend with other voices or instruments; performs with accurate intervallic relationships.					
performs with stylistic accuracy; accurately performs in the style(s) specified by the composer, arranger, or conductor.					
varies and adjusts timbre, motion, articulation, dynamics, and phrasing as needed or as specified by the composer, arranger, or conductor to construct an expressive performance.					
Comments:					

SA = Strongly Agree   A = Agree
PA = Partially Agree   D = Disagree
SD = Strongly Disagree

4. Extra-Musical

Sample Rubric for Assessing Classroom Protocol

Pathway						Destination
Assessment						
[name of student]	20 points / class					
	M	T	W	T	F	
Arrived to class on time – 4 pts.	N	Y	Y	Y	Y	Punctuality
Arrived to class with all required materials – 4 pts.	Y	N	Y	Y	Y	Preparedness
Did not interrupt the learning process for others – 4 pts.	Y	Y	Y	Y	N	Respect / Courtesy
Communicated respectfully with teacher and peers – 4 pts.	Y	Y	Y	Y	N	Respect / Courtesy
Participated fully – 4 pts.	Y	N	N	Y	N	Teamwork / Collaboration
Evaluation	16	12	16	20	8	72 / C

True or False?

Art resides in the quality of doing; process is not magic.

—CHARLES EAMES

VI

SIMPLICITY IS THE ULTIMATE SOPHISTICATION.

—LEONARDO DA VINCI

Inspired by the flagship texts, *Understanding by Design* (Wiggins and McTighe, 1998/2006) and *Results* (Schmoker, 1999), C–A–R–E represents distinct, yet interrelated processes for designing powerful units of study. Through authentic behaviors of distinct quality, the process of **Concentration** brings direction and focus—a milestone destination. In response, the processes of **Accommodation, Reflection,** and **Evaluation** define a student-centered pathway that is empowering, enriching, and revealing. The result is an Intensive CARE Unit (ICU)—educationally sound components working in concert, the sum of which is greater than their individual effects.

WHEN TRUE SIMPLICITY IS GAINED,

TO BOW AND TO BEND WE SHAN'T BE ASHAMED.

TO TURN, TURN WILL BE OUR DELIGHT,

'TIL BY TURNING, TURNING WE COME ROUND RIGHT.

ELDER JOSEPH BRACKETT, JR. (1848) • "SIMPLE GIFTS"

A. Professional lesson and rehearsal planning: An ICU is not only a compass for engineering the education prescribed in standards; it is equally a compass for creating lesson or rehearsal plans. In stark contrast to complex, disconnected, template-based treatises, lesson plans can evolve naturally in response to clear direction. Perhaps varying dramatically in form, a great lesson plan is now personal and defined by "yes" to simple questions:

- Will this plan be useful to me today?
- Will this plan maximize the time I have with my students?
- Will this plan help me equip students to navigate the paths that have been prescribed?
- Will this plan serve as a guide for implementing instructional strategies that are proven to be effective?

True or False?

An ICU is a root from which well-focused
lesson or rehearsal plans can grow.

B. Professional accountability: Through the process of **Reflection**, an ICU indicates clear connections with local priorities. It can also reveal curricular gaps or unnecessary redundances within a series of units or an entire program of study. Translation: professional accountability.

C. Professional record-keeping: Throughout a unit of study, each performance can potentially be recorded (entered into a grade book), which represents a "snapshot" of learning; a collection of snapshots creates a "scrapbook"

(Wiggins and McTighe, 2006). "Of course, Mrs. Jameson, I will be happy to show you how I arrived at Hannah's grade."

D. Professional collaboration: "Expecting teachers to do all of their own instructional planning, to gather and vet and refine their own materials entirely on their own is akin to expecting actors to not just act, but write all their own scripts" (Pogrow, 1996 as cited in Schmoker, 2001, p. 112). Imagine what could happen if music educators shared powerful lesson plans to create empowering and enriching pathways to common, adaptable unit-level objectives (milestones of emerging musicianship). The merger of "great ideas" brought to the table from experience, workshops, conventions, texts, journals, Internet resources, etc., could result in spectacular units of study. Literature, topics, themes, and prominent musicians could also be mapped—delineated throughout a program of study—to ensure engagement with diverse, exemplary, and developmentally appropriate content. In turn, teachers could take these plans and adjust them as needed to meet real-time learner and contextual needs. Thus, the process of designing ICUs is an invitation to exit the perils of isolation, to share expertise and experience, and to focus on measurable results with lasting value and consequence. The experts are among us; in case study after case study dramatic improvement begins with systematic, focused collaboration (Schmoker, 1999; Schmoker, 2001).

109

VII

WHEN I APPROACH A CHILD, HE INSPIRES IN ME TWO SENTIMENTS: TENDERNESS FOR WHAT HE IS AND RESPECT FOR WHAT HE MAY BECOME.

—LOUIS PASTEUR

Running parallel to the architecture of developing adaptive musical skills is differentiating between growth and achievement. When there is growth, there is achievement; when there is achievement, there is not necessarily growth. For example, when Erika tied her shoes this morning, she accomplished something: tied shoes. An important task was achieved. But did she grow from the process? Tying shoes was a skill she learned years ago, and it is likely Erika was thinking about something other than tying shoes as she engaged in the action of shoe tying. On the other hand, if she had successfully tied the laces into a new type of knot, there would have been two outcomes: growth (she can now tie a new knot) and achievement (tied shoes).

Similarly, if Tori types a letter using word processing software that she has used many times before, there is one outcome: a typed letter. If she learns to incorporate unfamiliar components to the letter (such as text boxes, clip art, borders, or shading), then there are two outcomes: growth and achievement.

If Iris journeys to a familiar destination down a well-traveled path, ultimately the only result is achievement. If her journey required conquering unknown challenges, such as scaling walls, repelling cliffs, or kayaking, she will have reached her destination (achievement) and learned new things in the process (growth).

Each of these analogies illustrates an important point: Achievement that does not result in new knowns is not growth. An accomplishment can be substantial, perhaps even fantastic, but if it's not new, then it's not growth. Fundamentally important to education is growth—development, advancement, or constructive change. This is not to say that achievement does not have value. Achievement is a pillar of society and central to all dimensions of education. Unless achievement occurs in conjunction with growth experiences, however, there is nothing new for students to draw upon or build upon as they move forward—the lasting value and consequence factor is diminished. Thus, exercising or applying knowledge (achievement) enriches today; introducing new knowledge or extending and refining pre-existing knowledge (growth) enriches tomorrow. The combination also moves music educators in directions away from anything that remotely resembles an activity director protected by the mask of education.

True or False?

When growth stops, erosion begins.

To engineer consequential growth and achievement, there is one—and only one—means of assurance: *discovery*.

THOUGHT ABOUT IT

NO DOUBT ABOUT IT

WHEN YOU SEEK YOU FIND

BRIAN MCKNIGHT • "COME BACK"

Casey can (kind of) read music that represents technical and interpretive demands at a grade 1 level. This is Casey's third year in band, and at the end of the preceding school year, she was playing the third trumpet part. Casey's favorite musician is Michael, the lead trumpet in the high school jazz band.

Christina is an exceptionally talented music-maker. This is only her second year of participation in band, but she practices daily and takes a thirty-minute flute lesson each week. Christina can sight-read music that represents technical and interpretive demands at a grade 2 level with a moderate degree of artistry. She was able to read near the specified tempo, incorporate most of the markings around the notes, and maintain clear, focused tone quality throughout the performance. Academically, Christina always makes As and is on track to graduate with a 4.0 GPA. When she's not studying or practicing, her interests include dancing, soccer, volleyball, visiting with her friends, and volunteering as a candy-striper at a local hospital. Her favorite musicians are Jean-Pierre Rampal and Justin Timberlake. Christina hopes to be a veterinarian some day and claims that her greatest weakness is "Guitar Hero."

If I were braver…
…I would challenge Michael for first chair.
…I would get my ears pierced anyway.
…I would quit doing what my friends do.
…I would say No!
…I would tell the truth.
…I would fight back.
…I wouldn't get any more scars.
…I would do something better than my brother for once.
…I would ask for help.

Robert is a gifted visual artist. Crowned the grand-prize winner of a statewide contest for young artists, however, wasn't enough to convince him. He says, "I don't know what the big deal is; it's just a picture."

Jamie is a licensed pilot. In a typical week, she goes to school, works a part-time job, and logs about 10 hours of flight time. Her dream is to become an astronaut. She is also more than happy to fly her director to away games.

Joseph is preoccupied with sports and fitness. Each morning he arrives to school early to work out and run the track. Recently, he began taking energy supplements to "bulk up."

These snapshots of *real* students represent a mere sampling of information that can potentially impact what, when, and how teachers teach and learners learn. As Bransford, Brown, and Cocking (2000) report,

Jane...
strong, quiet, clumsy, and independent;
daughter of Mary and James, or stepchild of Steve and Shari;
lover of my sister, privacy, and anything that gets me out of the house;
who feels lonely, lost, and almost always sick to my stomach;
who needs a hiding place, my own space, and Dr. Pepper;
who gives and gives and gives but isn't sure why;
who fears pain, decision-making, and getting fat;
who would like to see a movie, my older sister, and a new face in the mirror;
resident of planet earth
...Doe

[Students] come to formal education with a range of prior knowledge, skills, beliefs, and concepts that significantly influence what they notice about the environment and how they organize and interpret it. This, in turn, affects their abilities to remember, reason, solve problems, and acquire new knowledge. (p. 10)

Furthermore, "a sizeable number of students come into school with misconceptions about subject matter…and about themselves as learners (assuming they can't and never will be able to [sing], for example)" (McTighe and O'Connor, 2005, p. 14). Through discovery, however, teachers can circumvent misconceptions early, modify or enhance lessons to meet real-time learner needs…and sidestep potentially disastrous mistakes:

One afternoon, Ms. Hancock brought out a red wooden shoe and asked, "Who would like to earn a star for tying the shoe today?" My hand rocketed up, and my heart pounded with joy when she chose me. I pranced to the front of the room, took one lace, pinched it together to make a loop, and manipulated the other lace around the loop. I bent down and grabbed the shoelace with my teeth to pull it through the loop.

"Nasty Girl! What would your mother think of you putting that in your mouth?" bellowed Ms. Hancock. I had no answer. Emotionally shocked and ashamed, I silently retreated to the far end of the carpet and slumped to the floor…As I tried to make myself as small as possible, Ms. Hancock's ramblings about the filthy hands that had touched the laces and about never putting objects in your mouth became unintelligible to me. "Nasty girl" were the only words circulating in my mind, like a tornado gaining strength with nowhere to land. (Webb, 2000, p. 74)

This is an account of Kindergarten by teacher Linda Webb. She learned to tie shoes by watching her mother. By the way, her mother was born without hands.

AND TO BE HONEST

AT THE TIME

THOUGH I COULD SEE

I MUST HAVE BEEN BLIND

GILBERT O'SULLIVAN • "MY LOVE AND I"

Identifying students' background, prior knowledge, strengths, interests, and access to resources makes wise plans possible…even in large ensembles. Although it's much easier to teach "the band" instead of individual students, it's a stretch to assume that one can improve the ensemble's level of performance without really knowing the performance level of the individuals who make up the ensemble. In all contexts, and regardless of class size or circumstantial obstacles, to ask is to invite opportunity, and simple *inquiry* leads the way:

A. Who are you?

- **Bell work**

  I am best at…

  I would like to become better at…

  If I could change the world, I would…

  If I were braver…

- **Bio-poems**

  Line 1: First name

  Line 2: Four traits that describe you

  Line 3: Sibling of… (or Son, Daughter, Friend of…)

  Line 4: Lover of… (three people or ideas)

  Line 5: Who feels… (3 items)

  Line 6: Who needs… (3 items)

  Line 7: Who gives… (3 items)

  Line 8: Who fears… (3 items)

  Line 9: Who would like to see… (3 items)

  Line 10: Resident of…

  Line 11: Last name

- **"Tell me all about the person behind the name."**

  By the time I'm 25 I want to be rich.

  I don't think I'm very good at music.

  Listen and I will talk to you.

  Leave me out of class discussions…please!

  You can count on me.

- **Dear Mr. and Mrs. Jones,**

  The new school year is upon us and I am delighted to have your daughter in my class! Please help me to be the best teacher possible by sharing everything you can about Caitlin in "A Million Words or Less."

B. ADD? ADHD? Abuse? Divorce? Separation? Broken home? Illness? Disability? What modifications are needed to comply with IEP's? Who would benefit from a behavior contract? ELL? ESL?

- Consultation with colleagues

C. How accessible are essential resources, e.g., financial resources, emotional strength, mental capacity, spiritual guidance, physical health and mobility, external support systems, access to adult relationships/role models, and knowledge of the hidden rules associated within different socio-economic groups (Payne, 1996)?

- Consultation with colleagues

D. Are you a visual, auditory, verbal, physical, logical, social, or solitary learner?

- Learning style surveys

E. What do you already know?

Education is a journey "from a known, through the unknown, to a new known" (Boardman, 2001, p. 50); "we construct understanding of the world in which we live by synthesizing new experiences into what we have previously come to understand" (Brooks and Brooks, 1993, p. 52). Consequently, existing knowledge is the starting point from which all objectives must evolve.

What a student clearly "knows," regardless of what he or she "should" know according to standards or averages, is point A; point B (something new to learn) has a simple parameter: it must be related (associated, connected, linked) to what is "known." Otherwise, as Charlie Brown's teacher always said, "Wha-Wha...Wha-Wha-Wha-Wha."

> Teachers use [diagnostic assessments] to check students' prior knowledge and skill levels, identify student misconceptions, profile learners' interests, and reveal learning-style preferences. (McTighe and O'Connor, 2005, p. 11)

LET IT BE, LET IT BE

LET IT BE, LET IT BE

YEAH THERE WILL BE AN ANSWER, LET IT BE

THE BEATLES • "LET IT BE"

116

Investigation brings wisdom of unmatched quality. The more you learn about your students, the more you will see them (and treat them) as who they really are—people who have talents to mold, ideas to explore, strengths to expand, challenges to overcome, and dreams to pursue.

> Consider your own fingerprint, unlike any on earth, your unique signature. Can you think of a reason for evolution to produce such a signal unless the organism is one of a kind? And if you think of God instead of evolution, it will be even easier to deduce a purpose in all of this. If people are inherently sortable into a few categories…then the fingerprint is a crazy detail. It only makes sense as a guide to the individual experiment that each of us is. (Gatto, 1995, ¶ 25)

> Children come to school as integrated people with thoughts and feelings, words and pictures, ideas and fantasies. They are intensely curious about the world. They are scientists, artists, musicians, historians, dancers and runners, tellers of stories, and mathematicians. The challenge we face as teachers is to use the wealth they bring us. (Williams, 1983, pp. 189–190)

To be sure, students lose when allowed to hide; students win when teachers seek to find. But they are not alone. As William Arthur Ward reminds us, "When we seek to discover the best in others, we somehow bring out the best in ourselves."

Précis

In myriad of ways, effective teaching is "less about what the teacher does than about what the teacher gets the students to do" (Perkins, 1993, ¶ 29). In fact, the ultimate aim of teaching is governed by a simple premise: learning is something students must do for themselves; it is not something that can be done for them. Thus, when a program of study is defined by a progression of units that clearly and convincingly serve to develop and demonstrate comprehensive and adaptive musicianship, the architecture of music education takes potent form. In respect to ambitious intentions, ambition becomes clear, focused, measurable, empowering, enriching, and enlightening action—**Transformation**. A more credible and accountable demonstration of professionalism may not exist.

Questions for Reflection

- How do I know that my learners have learned?
- How are the methods I use to assess and evaluate learning worthy of a professional?
- How does the learning that occurs in my classroom relate to a K–12 program of study?
- How does the learning that occurs in my classroom reflect professional priorities?
- I'm a [band, orchestra, choir] director. How does designing units of study that develop and demonstrate the education prescribed in standards apply to me?
- What would happen if every music educator in my district met in teams at least twice a month to create common, adaptable ICUs?

destination: invitation

—MARTIN LUTHER, 1483–1546

Breakfast is where this journey begins. It's true! Several years ago, during a time when I was a semi-novice music educator doing super-novice music educator things, wretched hunger pains would frequent a stop at the famed golden arches. Unfortunately, my quick breakfasts were often far from beneficial to my waistline, which brought about an inevitable internal battle each time I approached the counter. Do I go for the bacon, egg, and cheese biscuit? Yum. Or do I settle for an Egg McMuffin, which has considerably less fat content? Not being a huge fan of poached eggs, the biscuit often won over the muffin because this preparation was far from pleasing to my palette, and as the battles continued, biscuits scored far ahead in terms of total orders made. One fine day in February, however, this ratio began a momentous reversal. As I waited for my order, it occurred to me that the stuff between the biscuit was my hang-up. I have no problem eating the healthier muffins, just a problem with the egg between the muffins. A breakthrough was near.

The next day I asked the server if I could substitute the egg on the muffin for the egg that came on the biscuit. She replied, "So you want a folded egg?" Ah, the secret was revealed! "Please," I replied, and the rest is history. With the very first bite I knew I was on to something big. Not only was this combination of breakfast food better for me, it was perhaps the greatest breakfast sandwich that I had ever tasted. Since that moment—my personal breakfast breakthrough—I have ordered nothing but an "Egg McMuffin with a folded egg." It's been a staple in my diet for years.

So what's the point? Consider the sandwich in original form. The sum total equals one English muffin, one piece of Canadian bacon, one slice of cheese, and one egg. In my customized version, the sum total equals one English muffin, one piece of Canadian bacon, one slice of cheese, and one egg. In terms of substance, they are identical. In terms of results, however, the difference is dramatic. The original preparation was far from attractive. I would give it attention (order it and eat it) only under great pressure to do the right thing. On the other hand, the new version became something completely inviting, something I repeatedly chose to order, without pressure, time and time again.

Believe it or not, this breakfast tale mirrors the work of many exemplary teachers. Moving from accuracy to fluency to competency in any mode of musical action takes time. Things that require time, especially in the age of instant gratification, are virtually one and the same as things that require motivation. In response, educators who consistently lead learners to significant displays of growth and achievement share a distinct expertise: the ability to invite participation, effort, enthusiasm, or even a desire to surpass expectations—***Destination: Invitation***.

From the sparks of conception to the echoes of completion, opportunities to learn are "made to order" with natural motivators that range from blatant displays of temptation to discrete, perhaps even hidden, incentives. Miles from mere tricks, hooks, or bait, the result is nothing less than spectacular— dynamic doing for doers to do.

in·vi·ta·tion
n a situation or action that tempts someone to do something or makes a particular outcome likely
(*invitation*, def. 1)

I

LIE DOWN AND LISTEN TO THE CRABGRASS GROW.

—MARYA MANNES

Based on extensive research, Strong, Silver, and Robinson (1995) report that "[students] who are engaged in their work are driven by four essential goals, each of which satisfies a particular human need" (p. 9):

Success: Work that enables learners to demonstrate and improve their sense of themselves as competent and successful.	
Curiosity: Work that stimulates learners' curiosity, awakening a desire for deep understanding.	Success breeds capacity—students become capable by being successful. Children are both problem solvers and problem generators; they not only attempt to solve problems presented to them, but they also seek and create novel challenges…One of the challenges of school is to build on children's motivation to explore, succeed, understand (Piaget, 1978) and harness it in the service of learning (Bransford, Brown, and Cocking, 2000, p. 102).
Originality: Work that permits learners to exercise and express their autonomy and originality, helping them to discover who they are and who they want to be.	
Relationships: Work that enhances learners' relationships with people they care about.	**True or False?** We only think when we are confronted with a problem.

Independently and in combination, and at all stages of development, responding to these needs invites learning *naturally.*

All students, to some extent, seek mastery, understanding, self-expression, and positive interpersonal relationships. But they are all different as well. Imagine what could happen if we engaged our students in a discussion of these four types of motivation. What might they tell us about themselves and their classrooms? Could we actually teach them to design their own work in ways that match their own unique potential for engagement? (p. 12)

Perhaps most important, as revealed through the following examples, tapping these powerful motivators is well within the reach of even the "busiest" educators.

A. Engineering success through differentiation (one size does not fit all): Steven was dedicated and persistent, but never really good at playing his cello. He had tried for years to make it out of last chair, but his skills were far from capable of taking him there. For test after test he would diligently practice, dreaming of the day "loser" wasn't code among his peers for "Steven."

Perhaps the most promising day came during his sophomore year. With four years of orchestra under his belt, Steven came within one point of scoring higher than Jill, a new freshman who recently switched from violin to cello. Steven was proud for getting so close, and with a smile on his face, he vowed to "get her next time." Sadly, the year concluded, as did his junior year, without change. Even his expensive new instrument didn't free him from last chair or the ridicule that lingered in tandem. In fact, Steven graduated as a seven-year holder of last chair. He did, however, receive a special service award at the annual banquet. His director surprised him with the award after a slide show that recapped the spring trip and the many awards and trophies the senior class had received. His parents were very proud and thought it was a great way to wrap up all of his years of service and participation. After all, Steven was dedicated and persistent, but never really good at playing his cello.

True or False?

I know Steven.

Holly was always passionate about music. When she was eight years old, her grandparents took her to see a concert at Powell Hall in St. Louis. She wasn't particularly interested in Britten's *War Requiem*, but she became captivated by a tall musician in the back. Throughout the concert, she followed his actions very carefully. She saw how he moved from instrument to instrument and was fascinated by his diverse talent. It was that very night when Holly decided that she, too, would like to be able to play those instruments. Everyone had always told her she had a natural sense of rhythm, and percussion seemed to be a natural fit.

On her ninth birthday, Holly's parents caved to her pleading and bought her a shiny pair of red drumsticks. She carried them everywhere, banging on everything she could. Despite the frequent teasing by her girlfriends, she continued to show interest in percussion. On her tenth birthday, Holly's parents surprised her with a drum set. The house was never the same. She played her new drums day and night. The radio was her band and she was the star. Her friends kept teasing, but she didn't care. She loved the sounds she was making and would play for anyone who would listen. Her parents remained skeptical, attributing her passion for percussion to "a phase." But Holly surprised them. She kept playing, she kept practicing, and she kept waiting for the day when she could finally play her drums with others.

About two years later, the day Holly had longed for arrived. Two music teachers visited her classroom, gave a short demonstration of brass, woodwind, and percussion instruments, and encouraged all of the students to sign up for band. Holly was first in line.

The first day of band class was slightly disappointing for Holly. She had envisioned that everyone else in the class would be as prepared as she was. She couldn't imagine why things were going so slow, but she hung in there. She just knew that once everyone got rolling, she would actually be part of the class.

As the days went on, Holly remained optimistic about her musical future, but pessimism slowly invaded her thoughts. She had been patient for so long, but as she put it, "All I ever get to play are baby tunes on a bell kit." She also despised the tiny mallets.

Midway through the second semester, Holly finally got a boost when her teacher passed out "real music" for their first concert. In fact, she grinned from ear to ear. Finally, she thought, a chance to do what the symphony musician did. As she looked at her part, however, she was curious about why she had so many rests. Her teacher told her that what the composer indicated was what she would have to do. And that was good enough for Holly because she just knew that eventually things would get more challenging, interesting, and inspiring. Thus, in song after song, and in concert after concert, Holly could be found smiling at the rear of the room behind her bass drum, patiently waiting for her three big notes. Occasionally she could even be found behind a triangle, waiting for her big moment to tap the obviously worn dinner bell.

Sadly, as the semesters went by not much changed and Holly grew tired of waiting to play. It seemed like every rehearsal was just another study hall for her. Sit, sit, sit. Wait, wait, wait. But, for what...to hit a drum once or twice every now and then? This was not what she had imagined. The symphony musician, she thought, must have been the world's most patient man. Holly's parents would frequently ask about her music class and her reply was always the same, "Oh, I don't know what we're supposed to be doing in that class. Usually I just do my homework or doze off for a while. It's so boring." Her parents, of course, didn't believe her, but she spoke the truth.

During the summer before her freshman year, Holly finally decided enough was enough. She replaced music with recreational sports in her schedule and found herself with much more time to hang out with her friends, who were amazed that she stuck with music so long anyway. Her percussion equipment, which had grown to a substantial size, was laid to rest in the back of her closet.

Holly is now 28 and remains passionate about music. She attends concerts, is obsessed with her iPod, and is famous for annoying her friends by singing along with the radio. In traffic jams and at stoplights, Holly is also frequently seen drumming on her steering wheel. It's moments like this when she thinks back to her days in school music, chuckling at the thought of becoming a percussionist.

True or False?

Good teaching is forever being on the cutting edge of a child's competence.

—Jerome Bruner

Teachers of performance-based classes are faced with a very real challenge: the dual charge of advancing the individual, but not at the expense of the group; advancing the group, but not at the expense of the individual. Fortunately, this can be easily accomplished through the design of unit-level objectives for both the ensemble and the individuals who create the ensemble, which parallels the practice of differentiation—creating different learning options in response to student needs.

Holly: In a live audition for the All-District Honor Band, Holly will perform the audition music with superior artistry.

Steven: After independent practice and peer tutoring, Steven will perform a series of grade 2 etudes with accurate pitch and rhythm at the specified tempos.

Class (including Holly and Steven): In live performance at the fall concert and the Pumpkin Festival, the students will perform [titles] with superior artistry.

Unfortunately, in many classrooms the focus is almost exclusively on the group—performance pressure prevails. The fact is forgotten that advancing the individual is effectively advancing the ensemble...poor Steven and Holly.

B. Engineering success by matching music to musicians (or problems to problem solvers):

In the context of performance-based school music classes, performing music artistically is prerequisite to any interpretation of success. When this takes too long to accomplish, however, the impatient alarm goes off. Enter boredom, frustration, and the like. Before you know it, the music-making journey becomes more of a battle of wills than a constructive union of music-makers. Instructional time

Readily attainable:
- Music that is readable.
- When performing the music for the first time, ranges, keys, rhythms, technical requirements are managed in a proficient manner.
- Mistakes occur, but without significant breakdowns.

Reasonably challenging:
- Music that provides an opportunity for the performer to explore something new.
- Music that expands upon previously acquired skills and/or concepts (e.g., a new key for a younger performer, a new meter for an intermediate musician, multiple tonguing demands for an advanced student).

inevitably becomes dominated with issues that are miles from anything productive or artistic. On the other hand, when learning becomes a hands-on tour of readily attainable and reasonably challenging performance demands, learners are given something they desperately need: a chance (Willingham, 2009).

126

Scenario 1: Performance unit in which the students study/perform five contrasting compositions. Each composition offers an appropriate musical stretch in relation to the median skill level within the group.	Scenario 2: Performance unit in which the students study/perform two contrasting compositions. One is far above the median level of the group in terms of technical and expressive demands. The other is far below the median level of the group.
Results	
Prime instructional time is spent teaching—making music. Rote teaching is minimal.	Rote teaching predominates. Depending on the song that is being rehearsed, students are either bored or frustrated.
Less time is required for learning the basic pitches and rhythms. The teacher has more time to teach higher-level performance concepts.	The teacher has little time for teaching anything but pitch and rhythm.
Students spend more time on task. As a result, misbehavior is deterred.	Due to boredom and frustration, a significant amount of instructional time is spent battling students for attention.
Students spend most of class time engaged in authentic musical actions; all students are active music-makers throughout rehearsals. Growth occurs through teacher influences and from each student's own experience.	Significant growth is stifled because more time is spent waiting to make music than actually making music.
Growth occurs in a smooth, linear manner.	Growth, when it occurs, comes from a jagged, labor-intensive journey that is riveted with stress and aggravation (for both students and conductor).
Deposit	**Withdraw**

- The principal of Hilltop High School has invited the band to perform at the Valentine's Day Pep Rally for Lonely Hearts. In support of growth, half of the music selected for the performance is familiar; the other half is new music that includes technical and interpretive demands that are attainable with a reasonable musical stretch. As a result, select arrangements of "Heartbreak Hotel," "My Funny Valentine," etc., serve as an effective means of extending and refining capacity as a music performer.

C. Engineering success and piquing curiosity through practice:

- Students in Mrs. Ahearn's choir begin the semester by preparing three compositions to perform at a naturalization ceremony. Following this performance, they learn three additional songs and perform all six in a joint concert with a local community choir. The semester concludes by preparing three more songs, and all nine compositions are then performed at a local nursing home, at the spring concert, and at the annual recording session to make a class CD. The challenge throughout is to make each and every rehearsal and performance better than the one before.

> Is a performance of exemplary repertoire, particularly an artistic performance, worthy of more than one presentation? Is a musical presented on only one night? How about an art exhibition, just one day? Would athletes work tirelessly and strenuously, commit to hundreds of hours of training and practice, and give up other interests just to play one or two games per season?

D. Engineering success and piquing curiosity through competition:

- Each semester, students in Ms. Kannon's band class compete for the following: first chairs, solo opportunities, student conductor opportunities, section leader positions, the Performer of the Year Award, the Most Improved Award, and the Above and Beyond Award.

- Convinced of the motivational power of competitive action, yet cautious not to instill the fear of losing, Mr. Slyman established an end-of-the-year solo competition. The contest is exclusive to the school district and open to all band, orchestra, and choir members.

The event is held on two consecutive evenings, adjudicated by a panel of volunteer musicians from the school and community. The winners even make the front page of the school and local newspapers.

Essential components of the program include (1) establishing a graded list of exemplary solo repertoire, (2) awarding medals in as many categories as possible, (3) maintaining, posting, and publicizing ongoing achievement records, (4) publicizing the event in as many ways as possible, (5) securing the services of accompanists, (6) obtaining the necessary audio equipment for recorded accompaniments, (7) obtaining the necessary recording equipment and personnel to create a DVD of each students' performance, and (8) making the thrust of the event a celebration of individual growth and achievement.

E. Engineering success by providing access to exemplary music:

- Ms. Staples' choir classes have access to a vast library of solo literature. Before and after school, student assistants supervise the checkout and return procedures.

F. Piquing curiosity through constructive challenges:

THERE'S A MOMENT WHEN FEAR AND A DREAM MUST COLLIDE

CIRQUE DU SOLEIL • "LET ME FALL"

- From memory, students at Madison Middle School work to perform all major scales accurately, in a slurred eighth note pattern, and in less than 60 seconds.

- At Sunset Elementary, students perform [titles] with accurate pitch and rhythm at the specified tempo to earn the black belt in recorder-karate.

- Students in Mrs. Wakefield's theory compose background music for commercials (announcements) produced by the student council to advertise upcoming events.

- Students in Ms. Olsen's class work in teams to create detailed production plans for a local charity's benefit concert.

- Students in Mr. Walberg's class attend local concerts and prepare comprehensive critiques of the performances. Many of these evaluations are included in the school's newspaper and all are posted on the school's website.

- Jacob's enrichment project is to produce a program for the local university radio station that showcases classic band literature and choral masterworks performed by regional bands and choirs; Makala prepares to audition for a concerto competition.

G. *Encouraging ownership and personalization; encouraging originality:*
Research findings compiled by the Northwest Regional Educational Laboratory (2005) underscore the virtues of creating goals that narrow students' focus while at the same time providing enough flexibility to facilitate ownership and personalization.

> Instructional goals should not be too specific. When goals are too narrowly focused they can limit learning. (Fraser, 1987; Walberg, 1999)

> If goals are stated in highly specific, behavioral objective format, they are not amenable to being adopted by students. (Marzano, Pickering, and Pollock, 2001, p. 95)

> Setting a goal too narrowly can focus students' attention away from other key material presented in class. Goals should be general enough

to allow students to personalize them. (Fraser, Walberg, Welch, and Hattie, 1987; Marzano, Pickering, and Pollack, 2001; Walberg, 1999)

130

If students are encouraged to personalize the teacher's goals, then learning increases. Student ownership enhances learning focus. Studies show the benefits of students setting sub-goals derived from the larger teacher-defined goals. (Bandura and Schunk, 1981; Morgan, 1985)

Creating opportunities for students to exercise and express their autonomy and originality is far from a complex proposition:

- Each semester, students in Mr. Popham's choir select their own solos or practice material from teacher-prescribed resources.

- During the "I'll Be Bach in a Minuet" unit, students in Ms. Zimmerman's class select their own masterwork to study.

- In Mrs. Denver's class, students select the artist(s) they would like to study in conjunction with a unit over Celtic music.

- Students in Ms. Davenport's class are free to use any style of music they like to compose a theme and variations.

- In conjunction with class learning activities, students in Mr. Listner's class complete a K–W–L (Know–Want to Know–Learned) chart for each topic of study.

- During rehearsals, students in Ms. Brown's orchestra are given frequent "practice time-outs" to improve personal sections or phrases of weakness.

- In conjunction with the Beethoven unit, students in Mrs. O'Meara's class work to answer to the following questions: What's so special about Beethoven? How does Beethoven and his music relate to me?

If students are challenged, if their interests in the subject matter are encouraged, if they are given autonomy support, then their intrinsic interests, their motivation for learning, and their test scores will all grow more effectively. (Sheldon and Biddle, 1998, p. 176)

What makes school a place that invites learning? According to Poplin and Weeres (1993), students want rigor and joy in their schoolwork, a balance of complexity and clarity, opportunities to discuss personal meanings and values, learning activities that are relevant and fun, and learning experiences that offer choice and require action.

H. Engineering cooperative learning; encouraging constructive relationships: Humans are innately social, and learning is enhanced through interaction with peers. Even a brief review of academic research reveals that students achieve at higher levels when given opportunities to learn with and from each other (Cunningham and Allington, 2006; Delpit, 2006). For teachers interested in engaging the learner, tapping into this natural motivator is just a wise decision away.

- Students in Mr. Jackson's high school orchestra tutor small groups of beginners to earn honors credit.

- Students in Mrs. Webster's eighth grade band practice in preparation for in-class duet recitals.

- During the first week of the term, Mrs. Wagener divides her high school choir into quartets. At the spring concert, each quartet performs "in front of the curtain" as the spectrum of choirs from throughout the program move on and off the stage.

- To advance her students' ability to perform music artistically, Mrs. Eldredge allows her students to choose practice material from a collection of music that is grouped in levels from 1–10. Each level contains a diverse array of solos, etudes, exercises, and duets with similar technical and interpretive demands (keys, rhythms, range, tempo, etc.). After successfully performing five compositions from the appropriate base level, students must then pass a corresponding sight-reading exercise before moving on to the next level. All of this occurs in conjunction with class music-making activities.

1st Hour	*1*	*2*	*3*	*4*	*5*	Sight-Reading	*1*	⇨
Kylie	Level 2 ☑	Level 2 ☑	Level 2 ☑	Level 2 ☑	Level 2 ☑	Level 2 ☑	Level 3 ☑	⇨
Kevin	Level 1 ☑	Level 1 ☑	Level 1 ☑	Level 1 ☑	Level 1 ☑	Level 1 ☑	Level 2 ☑	⇨

Throughout the spectrum of grade levels, the power of natural motivators is central to exceptional curricular design.

Success:	How is the unit aligned with the learners' stage of development, interests, and/or needs?
Curiosity:	How will the unit stimulate effort, interest, and participation?
Originality:	How will the unit encourage ownership and personalization?
Relationships:	How does the unit create opportunities for students to develop or strengthen relationships with people they care about?

II

As I was sitting in my chair,

I knew the bottom wasn't there,

Nor legs nor back, but I just sat,

ignoring little things like that.

—Hughes Mearns

Have you ever been in a conversation where the other person wouldn't stop talking, even though he really had nothing to say? Have you ever received a voicemail where the caller rambled on and on, seemingly forever, before getting to what you really wanted: the phone number? Have you ever sat through a marathon workshop where the speaker was obviously passionate about minutiae? This is not one of those times.

A. All students deserve the best possible music education.

> Because of the role of the arts in civilization, and because of their unique ability to communicate the ideas and emotions of the human spirit, every American student, pre-K through grade 12, should receive a balanced, comprehensive, sequential, and rigorous program of instruction in music and the other arts. This includes students in public schools, private schools, and charter schools, as well as home-schooled students. (MENC, 1997, Where We Stand: The Role of Music in American Education: Access to Music Education, no. 1)

B. It is the right of every child to receive a balanced, comprehensive, sequential music education taught by qualified music teachers (MENC Centennial Congress, 2007, ¶ 1).

> The mission of MENC is to advance music education by encouraging the study and making of music by all. (MENC, 2008, banner)

C. *Change in the way teachers approach music education is inevitable.*

We are challenged to reconstruct our profession so it can function effectively in today's and tomorrow's musical worlds rather than yesterday's…if we do not grow and change we will never be anything more than we presently are, going our own way, serving the needs of the few, desperately trying to persuade people to support us fully nevertheless, and continuing to be frustrated by their reluctance to do so…We must get over the outdated and unrealistic assumption that performance is the one, singular, royal road to being musical and being an effective music educator. (Reimer, 2004, pp. 36–37)

D. *Plan B is inevitable; misery is optional.*

Every secondary school should offer courses for those students who are interested in music but who, for lack of ability, background, or time, do not participate in band, orchestra, or chorus. The curriculum should include a broad array of opportunities for learning diverse genres of music in diverse settings, at least some of which have no prerequisites. (MENC, 1994, p. 5)

It is completely unrealistic and unfair to performance—[bands, orchestras, choirs]—to expect it to fulfill what the Standards demand—a comprehensive representation of specialized learning opportunities, each with its own veracity. The time required in performance programs to accomplish what they are responsible for—heightened intelligence and creativity in the performer role—allows only sporadic attention to the other roles. If we do not

NASA DID NOT SEND MEN TO THE MOON BY BUILDING ON THE CHASSIS OF A MODEL T.

—JUDITH LLOYD YERO

grow and change we will never be anything more than we presently are, going our own way, serving the needs of the few, desperately trying to persuade people to support us fully nevertheless, and continuing to be frustrated by their reluctance to do so. (Reimer, 2004, pp. 36–37)

Our curriculum must reflect more than our own desires; it must reflect the needs and desires of the students we serve…We need to develop programs that are flexible and of greater variety than those currently in use in most schools…We need electives as broad and diverse as the interests and enthusiasms of our students. (MENC Centennial Congress, 2007, ¶ 3)

When opportunities to learn embrace widespread musical interests and enthusiasms, the nature of music education reflects the cultural and social milieu in which it exists (Kratus, 2007). Furthermore, when content mastery is not the aim of music education, but rather the means of music education, the pathway is only significant in terms of how many students it invites to travel. In the end, it all comes down to a single question: In addition to what we teach, is teaching for meaning in any way connected to who we reach?

True or False?
Love all; serve all.

E. Complete music education requires some degree of involvement in all three artistic processes: (1) performing music, (2) creating music, and (3) responding to music. In virtually all publications that set forth standards, there is a clear consensus. As the authors of the Indiana Academic Standards for Music (2007) prescribe, for example, all musical processes should be "addressed to some extent in all courses across the music curriculum, with the primary focus of a class resulting in the prominence of some and less emphasis on others" (p. i). The same premise holds true, perhaps more realistically, within the scope of a program of study—students should be given opportunities to engage in all three musical (artistic) processes. Eventually, however, the primary focus must become one mode of musical action with ancillary emphasis on the others. The parameter of time, or the limited amount of time that is generally and realistically available, dictates few other options. Besides, is a high school graduate with the ability to *kind of* perform music artistically, create music effectively, and respond to music competently something that glows with significance? If not, consider, for example, a K–12 design (shown at the right) that gave equal emphasis to all musical processes in the elementary grades and then offered two specialized tracks in the secondary grades, each of which focused primarily on one mode of musical action with ancillary emphasis on the others.

Grade Level	Course	Emphasis	Required Space
Elementary	Music	Performing music Creating music Responding to music	Music room Traditional classroom
Secondary Track 1	Band(s) Orchestra(s) Instrumental Ensembles Choir(s) Vocal Ensembles	Performing music Responding to music Creating music	Rehearsal room
Secondary Track 2	Music	Responding to music Creating music Performing music	Rehearsal room Traditional classroom Computer lab

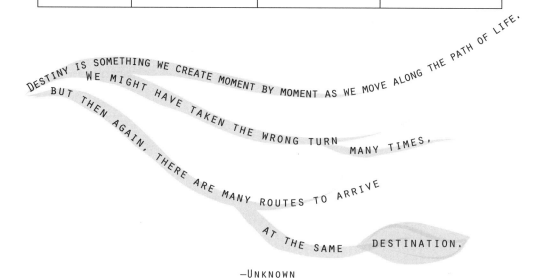

DESTINY IS SOMETHING WE CREATE MOMENT BY MOMENT AS WE MOVE ALONG THE PATH OF LIFE. WE MIGHT HAVE TAKEN THE WRONG TURN MANY TIMES, BUT THEN AGAIN, THERE ARE MANY ROUTES TO ARRIVE AT THE SAME DESTINATION.

—UNKNOWN

136

F. The content embedded in a topic or theme is the medium for sparking, extending, or refining the macro-skills of musicianship. The possibilities are vast. In performance-oriented programs of study, a series of performances naturally defines a series of units. In non-performance-oriented programs of study, a series of *topics or themes* is a highly effective means of organizing and constructing units of study.

EVERYONE WHO'S EVER TAKEN A SHOWER HAS AN IDEA. IT'S THE PERSON WHO GETS OUT OF THE SHOWER, DRIES OFF, AND DOES SOMETHING ABOUT IT WHO MAKES A DIFFERENCE.

—NOLAN BUSHNELL

1. Imagine that you are a recent graduate of Novel High School who participated in Mrs. Parker's music classes since the sixth grade. These are the units of study that sparked, extended, or refined your ability to perform, create, read, notate, analyze, describe, evaluate, and relate music.

American Masters
Anniversaries
Are You Scared?
Because Grammy Said So
Bernstein
Can I Borrow Your Playlist?
Colors
Composers
Connections: Art-Music-
Literature
Contemporary Jazz
Continental Divides
Copy Rights and Wrongs
Cultural Phenomenon
Decades of Change
Emotional Masterpieces
Eras
Fire
Form-ulas
Garage Bands

Global Rhythms
Guitar Heroes
Hip-Hop
History of Jazz
Holidays
I'll Be Bach in a Minuet
I've Got the Blues
I Want My MTV
Kings and Queens of Pop
Latin America Popular
Music
Let the Spiritual Move You
Modern Alternatives
Modern Masters
Music ala MP3
Music and Imagination
Music Con Brio
Music in Animated Film
Music in Film
Music in the Dark Ages

Music of Folk
Musical Inventions
Name that Tune
Opera Theatre
Outer Space
Patriotism
Renaissance Men
Reunions
Seven Wonders of the
Musical World
Songs of the Earth
Soul Sounds
Soundtracks
The American Musical
The Magic of Mozart
The Music of Our Lives
Timeless Treasures
"West Side Story"
Worlds of Music
Virtuosity

True or False?

Applying the "built–brought–behind" strategy to these topics
could yield highly consequential outcomes.

2. Imagine that you're a third grader in Mrs. Pena's class. The following units of study frame the year in music:

- Cracking the Code – performing music with an emphasis on reading rhythms
- What's Your Pulse? – performing music with an emphasis on tempos and tempo maintenance
- Do You Hear What I Hear? – analyzing music for the elements of music
- Tribal Rhythms – reading and performing music in a drum circle
- Rhyme Time – creating melodies, lyrics, and instrumental accompaniments
- Karate Musicale – performing increasingly diverse and sophisticated music to reach the "black belt" level

3. Imagine participating in Mr. Marshall's music class. This is where you learn to:

- "Create music effectively" by using notation software to compose music that mirrors and enhances a self-recorded, one-minute video clip – *The Music Video.*
- "Relate music comprehensively" by exploring the roles of various musicians within the production of an animated film – *How'd They Do That?*
- "Analyze and describe music effectively" by using a score excerpt (e.g., *Batman* by Elfman) to identify several ways in which the elements of music are used to enhance parallel scenes in the film – *The Secrets of the Score.*

4. Imagine participating in Mrs. Patrick's Earth Grooves class. Students explore world music and cultures via the dance—salsa, tango, samba, paso doble, jive…ad infinitum.

5. Imagine completing the Human Voice unit in Ms. Winter's music class. Students explore a specific genre or style of music through the preparation of self-selected, representative solos or duets. Warm-ups, diction studies, and sight-singing support the development of performance fundamentals, while frequent, comprehensive evaluations of peer performances extend students' understanding of the criteria by which music-making is labeled exceptional, superior, or artistic. The unit concludes with a recording session to make a class CD.

> How do singers communicate the meaning of a song?
> What should singers do to take care of their voices?
> What themes and elements make good lyrics?
> What should a singer look for when selecting a new song to learn?
> Why should you care about what you look like when you're singing?
>
> (adapted from Thompson, 2007, p. 39)

6. Imagine participating in Ms. Nichols' class—Music in America: A Mosaic. In this class the students' abilities to create music, analyze and describe music, evaluate music and music performance, and relate music is integrated, extended, and refined through a series of units based on Grammy Award-winning songs and artists in diverse categories. (FYI: In 2006, there were 108 Grammy Award categories.)

7. Imagine that you're a student at Allegro Middle School where Mr. Breckenridge, a veteran band director, created Planet Percussion, an exploratory course in which all students are welcome to explore global rhythms. The curriculum focuses on world music and drumming in conjunction with curricula for geography and history. Piano Lab and Class Guitar are also offered, completing the trio of the most popular instruments on Earth.

140

In a study that included 163 Florida band directors, Juchniewicz (2007) reports the following findings about the implementation of non-traditional music classes: Jazz Ensemble, Music Theory, and Percussion Ensemble were the top three preferred courses, while Mariachi Ensemble, Bluegrass Ensemble, and Irish Fiddling were the three least preferred courses. (abstract)

8. *Imagine* participating in Mr. Pennington's Digita Musica class. Students work in teams to create anthologies that are organized by genre. Subscriptions are purchased, songs are downloaded, CDs are burned, and extensive research into the genre and its artists are presented in the form of album notes.

9. *Imagine* attending Accelerando High School, where you are welcomed and encouraged to participate in The Art of Making Art, a special semester-long course (inspired by Broadway and *Blast!)* that celebrates and sparks continued interest in the fine and performing arts.

Open to any student that has a passion for the arts, the focus of this multi-dimensional experience is simple: live, artistic fusion (see Appendix B). At the first meeting, Ms. Fuller, who also directs the choir, tells the students, "We are artists. Singing, dancing, designing, painting, playing instruments, building, acting, expect to do it all. In the end, you'll be an important part of a production so spectacular that words could never do it justice...it must be experienced."

Creators, performers and others involved in the production and presentation of the arts include painters, composers, choreographers, playwrights, instrumentalists, singers, dancers, actors, conductors, costumers, directors, and lighting designers. (MENC, 1994, p. 25)

The process begins with collective brainstorming and design sessions, and evolves into a spectacular showcase of students' talents. When the production reaches its final form, everyone contributes, everyone is important, and all are connected to something larger than themselves. Students share the work, lasting friendships are formed, and new insights into all that is explicit and implicit to "artistry" take shape. For the audience, which ranges from peers to parents to patrons, there is something for everyone.

141

True or False?

Imagination continually frustrates tradition…

that is its function.

—JOHN PFEIFFER

PRÉCIS

Call it a joy or a consequence of teaching. Either way, motivation is not a choice. As long as students are breathing, "invitations to learn" will always be in style. For teachers on the front lines of music education, this means the journey of **Invitation** must follow two distinct paths: one for the students you know today, another for the students you have yet to meet.

QUESTIONS FOR REFLECTION

- How do the pathways to musicianship in my classes stimulate participation, effort, enthusiasm, or even a desire to surpass expectations?
- How do I honor diversity?
- How am I moving music education forward?
- What would happen if every music educator in my district met in teams at least twice a month to design common, adaptable, and *dynamic* ICUs?

- What would happen if we used assessment data from these ICUs to continually refine the curriculum?
- What would happen if we applied this process to new and innovative courses that encourage the study and making of music by all?

True or False?

It is easy to dodge our responsibilities,

but we cannot dodge the consequences of dodging our responsibilities.

—Sir Josiah Stamp

destination: illumination

Sometime in the twentieth century the legendary Madeline Hunter described a vexing predicament:

> How do I make Johnny learn? is a question that has plagued all teachers since the beginning of time. The answer is simple. It can't be done! No one can make a child or anyone else learn.

Sometime circa 470–399 BC, Socrates proposed the solution:

> I cannot teach anybody anything.
> I can only make them think.

Even the best-laid plans have their downfalls. Unequalled education is explicitly human and tied to instruction. Although the term "instruction" is frequently used as a synonym for just about all facets of a teacher's practice, *in* practice, however, instruction is when teachers "go live" (i.e., real-time interaction between teacher and learners).

At its best, the impact of instruction can be nothing short of staggering. Given the inexorable diversity among learners, however, exemplary instruction is always defined by the moment. "Like improvisers, music educators engaged in specific teaching-learning situations exhibit their musical and educational expertise in relation to highly complex contexts that have their own tempos, rhythms, designs, and expressions of emotion (Elliot, 1995, p. 257). Indeed, effective instruction is far from suited to the faint-hearted. Instructional brilliance—***Destination: Illumination***—is the work of teachers who are expert at matching tactic to task and method to minds.

Accordingly, and in support of *results as best practice*, the wisdom to follow explores versatile principles that can be applied to almost all instructional scenarios. The intent is not to diminish established methods of instruction or strategies gleaned from study, experience, or professional development. These ideas have a much simpler purpose: to complement them.

144

I

WELCOME BACK MY FRIENDS

TO THE SHOW THAT NEVER ENDS

WE'RE SO GLAD YOU COULD ATTEND

COME INSIDE, COME INSIDE

EMERSON LAKE AND PALMER • "KARN EVIL 9 FIRST IMPRESSION"

For most learners, the impetus to learn does not come from content, but rather because a teacher has made the content inviting (Knight, 2006; Strong, Silver, and Robinson, 1995; Tomlinson 2002). To this end, piquing attention at the *onset* of instruction encourages mental engagement; piquing attention *throughout* instruction helps the learner to remain engaged. The possibilities are vast:

- Demonstrate musical artistry.
- Describe a fascinating fact.
- Display an optical illusion.
- Initiate a challenge.
- Perform a magic trick.
- Play a practical joke.
- Play an audio or video clip.
- Play a recording from the day before.
- Present a mind trick.
- Pose a mystery.
- Reveal a startling statistic.
- Share a personal experience.
- Stir emotions.

> Jim was just not acting like himself. He did *not* want to go home. He said he was afraid to go home because of the man in the mask. What do you think he means? *(pause)* What if I told you that Jim was on third base?

Healthy emotions—such as concern, excitement, anticipation, or suspense— are doorways to attention and memory.

> Our emotional system drives our attention system, which drives learning and memory and everything else that we do. It is biologically impossible to learn and remember anything that we don't pay attention to. The emotional system tells us whether a thing is important—whether we ought to put any energy into it. (Sylwester as cited in D'Arcangelo, 1998, p. 25)

> The stronger the emotion connected with an experience, the stronger the memory of that experience. Chemicals in the brain send a message to the rest of the brain: "This information is important. Remember it." (Wolfe & Brandt, 1998, p. 13)

IT'S AWFULLY CONSIDERATE OF YOU TO THINK OF ME HERE

AND I'M MUCH OBLIGED TO YOU FOR MAKING IT CLEAR

PINK FLOYD • "JUGBAND BLUES"

Another effective strategy for grabbing attention is to clarify learning… not doing, but learning. This is central to all interpretations of exemplary instruction. Students want to know *why* they should do the doing prescribed for them to do (Why should I do this? How will this help me?). Imagine what could happen if objectives are left open for interpretation.

What did you learn in music this year?
- "I don't know."
- "I don't know…songs and stuff."
- "I told you…singing!"
- "I learned the staff: f–a–c–e."
- "I learned the staff: f–a–c–e. Oh, and every good boy does fine."
- "Sometimes we learn new songs, but we mostly just watch old movies that have lots of singing."

- "I'm really good at selling stuff. Look at all these cool prizes I won."
- "I'm not sure music is for me. No way will I ever be as good as this kid named Josh.
- "How to start, stop, and sit a while."
- "We learned this really hard song, but I don't remember the name."
- "Orlando is amazing."
- "Music takes way too much time."

II

JUST REMEMBER IN THE WINTER FAR BENEATH THE BITTER SNOW LIES THE SEED THAT WITH THE SUN'S LOVE IN THE SPRING BECOMES THE ROSE

BETTE MIDLER • "THE ROSE"
SONGWRITER: AMANDA MCBROOM

There is widespread agreement that seamless congruity should exist between objectives, assessment, and instruction (Cawelti, 1995; Gaddy, Dean, and Kendall, 2002; Guskey and Schultz, 1996; Marzano, 2007; Nitko and Brookhart, 2006; Schmoker, 1999; Wiggins and McTighe, 2006); the cornerstones of a teacher's practice should be well matched in content and focus. For example, if the objective is performing music artistically, a congruent instructional plan involves a great deal of modeling. If the objective is sight-reading music proficiently, congruent instruction should involve guiding students through the steps a skilled reader takes prior to performing new music. For students to score 100% on a quiz over musical terms, congruent instruction consists of frequent review and application of the terms. In all cases, effective instruction is defined by what it takes to equip the learners to successfully achieve a clear, predetermined objective. This is illuminating—informative, revealing—instruction in brilliant color. This is also the antidote to random acts of teaching.

True or False?

The following scenario would never occur.

Objective	performing music artistically
Assessment & Evaluation	attendance, punctuality, and participation
Instruction	telling groups of students how to fix performance errors

III

SHOW ME THE WAY

SHOW ME THE WAY

GIVE ME THE STRENGTH AND THE COURAGE TO BELIEVE THAT I'LL

GET THERE SOMEDAY

AND PLEASE SHOW ME THE WAY

STYX • "SHOW ME THE WAY"
SONGWRITER: DENNIS DEYOUNG

Ben and Sam have 180 days to prepare for their first marathon.

Ben meets with his coach once every three weeks. At each meeting, they stretch, warm up, and run together. During these progressively longer runs, they practice endurance, pacing, and breathing techniques. At every other meeting they also go to the grocery store together to select nutritious meals and snacks. About a month ago, the coach even met him at the shoe store.

Sam meets with his coach once a week to get advice and feedback about his conditioning, pace, endurance, nutrition, rest, footwear, and apparel

Which runner will be best prepared to complete the race?

I HEAR AND I FORGET.

I SEE AND I REMEMBER.

I DO AND I UNDERSTAND. ⇨ ⇨ ⇨   I do with an expert....

—CHINESE PROVERB   ⇩

148   I hear much better.

I see much clearer.

I understand much faster.

Perhaps the most versatile of all instructional strategies is "guided practice."

> Although [guided practice] is most commonly associated with the work of Madeline Hunter, it has a rich tradition and theory base stemming from Vygotsky's work in the zone of proximal development and the more recent work on scaffolding. Vygotsky (1978) hypothesized that a learner needs the most guidance when working in the zone of development in which she has not yet acquired a skill [the ability to do something well] but has some initial idea of it—in effect, when the learner is shaping a procedure she has been introduced to…[S]caffolded instruction is, at its core, guiding a learner through the shaping of a skill or process. (Marzano, 1992, p. 60)

> There are, in the end, only two main ways human beings learn: by observing others (directly or vicariously) and by trying things out for themselves. Novices learn from experts and from experience. That's all there is to it. Everything else is in the details. (Meier, 1995, p. 181)

Guided practice comes in many forms, and the versatility of this strategy makes it adaptable to a host of teaching-learning contexts.

A. *Modeling; live example; demonstration:* In *The Nature of Expertise,* Duke and Simmons (2006) present a vivid description of guided practice in the context of music performance:

[Expert] teachers play examples from the students' repertoire to demonstrate important points. The teachers' modeling is exquisite in every respect. In all instances in which the teachers demonstrate, whether singing, gesturing, or playing, they embody the expressive elements of the music while executing the example nearly flawlessly. [Additionally,] the teachers often juxtapose a remarkably faithful imitation of the student's performance with their model of the performance goal…(¶ 21)

Carla's teacher creates a vivid mental picture of the appropriate style for "Irish Tune from County Derry" by performing the music on her primary instrument.

Barry's teacher explains that "a smooth, connected style" is appropriate for "Irish Tune from County Derry."

Before and after school, Mrs. Spencer teaches lessons two at a time. She pairs students based on instrumentation, interests, and skill levels. Mrs. Spencer's instrument is always nearby because each lesson ends with a trio performance.

B. *Guiding practice with guiding questions:*

Posture/Position	• How does it feel to stand perfectly straight?
Inhalation	• How does it feel when you take a really big breath?
Exhalation	• What does releasing a really big breath remind you of?
Tone Quality	• What words best describe your tone in that performance?
Technique	• Why is this fingering more efficient than this one? • When should this technique be applied?
Rhythm	• Why do we say that rhythm is something you feel? • How many eighth notes did you feel when you performed that whole note?
Articulation	• How does the tongue move to produce a legato phrase?
Expression	• Why is this version more expressive than the previous one?

150

C. Whole-part-whole instruction:

In acting, we rehearse a few lines of dialogue, then put them back into Act 2, Scene 4, and rehearse again as needed. In writing, we fine-tune our story introduction, read the whole story to see if it all works, and then have the work peer edited. Alas, the introduction confuses the reader, so we work on it again. Similarly, in basketball, we practice shooting and dribbling in isolation, work on drills that combine the two, and then have a controlled scrimmage to see if we can put everything together in context. On the basis of the feedback from results in the whole performance, we go back to drill work to overcome misunderstandings, bad habits, or forgotten lessons. We constantly recycle through work on specific elements, chunks of performance, and performance as a whole. (Wiggins and McTighe, 2006, p. 251)

"The technical demands in this passage are based on the Ab major scale, so let's practice this scale for a while…Okay, let's go back to the solo and try that phrase again."

"Great! You performed that passage much more accurately. What else needs attention? Right! We're losing tempo. Let's go back to the scale, but this time we'll play it with the metronome… Okay, we're ready to try that passage again."

IV

NEVER MIND…

THE WORDS I THOUGHT I BROUGHT I LEFT BEHIND

SO NEVER MIND

THE REPLACEMENTS • "NEVER MIND"
SONGWRITER: PAUL WESTERBERG

Learning is the result of thinking, of being mentally engaged. Thus, the more students think about something, the more likely they are to remember that something. For teachers, the corollary of this wisdom is that strategic feedback is fuel for thought. Extending and refining skills and understandings requires extensive and focused thinking in the form of practice that is united with and guided by frequent and thought-provoking feedback (Chappuis and Stiggins, 2002; Marzano, Pickering, and Pollock, 2001; McTighe and O'Connor, 2005; Rosenshine, 1997).

151

A. *Thought-provoking feedback:*

Problems to Solve	*Answers to Remember*
See if you can determine exactly where the tempo is changing.	You're rushing; you're dragging.
How are you blending with those around you?	You're sharp; you're flat; you're too loud.
What style do you think best fits here?	Make the notes longer.
What changes from A to B?	You missed the key change.
The note has a dot over it. What do you think this means in this phrase?	The note has a dot over it. Make it shorter.
Is what you're doing working? What do you think we should try now?	That's not working. Try this…
Are you satisfied with the results? Why?	I'm not satisfied with this.
Let's pick it back up at letter G. I'm listening for flawless intonation and dynamic contrast from the land of "issimo," not "ezzo."	Let's pick it back up at letter G.

To be most effective, teacher response to learner performance—feedback—should be criterion-referenced, or connect learner thinking to a specific level of skill or knowledge (Marzano, Pickering, and Pollock 2001). In least effective form, teacher response to learner performance—feedback—is a high whistling or howling noise caused by a loud speaker.

B. Criterion-referenced feedback:

Criteria	Criterion-Referenced Feedback *That was good because…*
Maintains appropriate body and/or instrument position.	…you maintained correct instrument and body position throughout the performance.
Performs with a resonant, focused, and projecting tone, regardless of range or dynamic level.	…you maintained a full, characteristic tone quality throughout the performance.
Performs with accurate intervallic relationships; when applicable, adjusts tone, pitch, and volume to blend with others.	…you adjusted the pitch.
Performs pitches and rhythms accurately and with synchrony to an appropriate pulse; when applicable, performs at a steady tempo.	…you maintained a steady tempo; you didn't slow down this time.
Performs with stylistic accuracy; accurately performs in the style(s) specified by the composer, arranger, or conductor.	…each phrase was articulated correctly.
Varies and adjusts timbre, tempo, articulation, dynamics, and phrasing as needed or as specified by the composer, arranger, or conductor to construct an expressive performance.	…you created a sense of tension in the phrase through dynamic contrast and a slight ritardando.

C. Too much feedback: Have you ever felt like you and a handful of students are the only ones who care about performing well? Perhaps the lack of stimulating (thought-provoking) feedback is partially to blame. Feedback in the form of "answers to remember" often accompanies the notorious "fix-it" approach, a style of teaching/rehearsing by band, orchestra, and choral directors in which students begin performing, are quickly stopped, and then sit a while as the director rambles a variety of "fixes." This tactic is equivalent to the "start–stop–sit-a-while strategy" and translates into "I am here to perform what my teacher tells me, when he tells me, and how he tells me…I wonder what's for lunch today" in the minds of many (if not most) students in the ensemble. Such tactics do not encourage student ownership in the music-making process but rather passive involvement as "the teacher is always solely responsible for decision-making…and the students act as mere automatons with little independent thought" (Apfelstadt, 1989, p. 74). Through consistent use of stimulating feedback, however, the students are prompted to work together and become active participants. In contrast to a one-man show, stimulated minds work in concert to pursue superior levels of performance; "effectiveness becomes more of a function of the degree to which the conductor and group become one in their mission" (Armstrong and Armstrong, 1996. p. 25). As a bonus for students, a collaborative effort to make things "right" is welcome relief from continually being caught "wrong."

D. Effective and ineffective feedback:

> Does your feedback tell students what to think, how to think, or that they can think? (Tomlinson, 2002)

[–] Mrs. McGurk cheerfully assists Maya with her solo by showing her trill fingerings, singing confusing rhythms, and clapping like a metronome. By thinking for her, Mrs. McGurk helps Maya to get through a song.

[+] Mr. Buck cheerfully assists Noah with his solo by prompting him to look up fingerings in his method book, encouraging him to count out confusing rhythm passages (like prompting a young reader to sound out a confusing word), and recording him for self-evaluation of tone, tempo, etc. By assisting him to think for himself, Mr. Buck leads Noah down the path of musical independence.

[–] In response to incorrect rhythmic performance, Mrs. Nolen tells the bewildered cellos to "subdivide."

[+] In response to incorrect rhythmic performance, Mr. Bryant "thinks aloud" by explaining the process he uses to demystify a complex rhythmic passage.

E. Vague feedback: Yoheved Kaplinsky, chair of the piano department at The Juilliard School, proposes that "a varied vocabulary [is necessary] to express the same idea with different students."

154

The term "musical," which is prevalent throughout the music education enterprise, however, is not among the best. What does this word specifically imply? In the mind of a fourteen-year-old, for example, what does "Your performance needs to be more musical" mean? Likely something similar to this: "My performance was kind of good, but I need…uhh…more practice."

> **Best response to a poor performance:** ☺
> "I like the end of the song…the end. You know, when the song ends and you come to a stop…I love that."
> —William Shatner (playing American Idol's Simon Cowell) in Brad Paisley's *Celebrity* video
> **Poor response to a best performance:** That was very musical.

F. Incomparable feedback: "Reinforcing effort can help teach students one of the most valuable lessons they can learn—the harder you try, the more successful you are" (Marzano, Pickering, and Pollock, 2001, p. 59). For example, in response to Jillian's composition, Mr. O'Briant exclaims, "See! All that time you invested after school has really paid off. This is very powerful music and I can't wait for you to share it with the rest of the class. They will be so impressed."

G. The potential of feedback: People behave according to how they feel, not what they know. For example, consider the following: "I can't seat you for thirty minutes" or "In thirty minutes I will have a wonderful table for you" (Marshall, 2001, ¶ 3). The message is the same, but the response will likely be very different.

True or False?
The repercussions of applying optimism and positivity to all teacher-student interactions could be monumental.

H. Non-verbal feedback Few things stimulate effort more than positive recognition. Accordingly, Mr. Donovan is an active publicist. Student accomplishments are frequently recognized on the daily announcements, in the school and community papers, on the sign in front of the school, in the yearbook, on bulletin boards in the main hallways, on the school's website, on the district's website, and during half-time announcements at athletic events. The printed program for the annual spring concert is also a showcase for individual and collective student achievements. Additionally, Mr. Donovan spotlights the work of dozens of students each week through "Rave Reports" on his classroom home page.

155

V

POLICE • "SYNCHRONICITY I"

To learn anything effectively, new information must be linked to existing knowledge; every encounter with something new requires the brain to fit the new information into an existing knowledge structure or neural network. As Brooks and Brooks (1993) report, "We construct understanding of the world in which we live by synthesizing new experiences into what we have previously come to understand" (p. 52). Consequently, teachers have just two options when it comes to introducing new information: (a) connect new information to prior knowledge/experience or (b) create a connecting or revealing experience with them (Westwater and Wolfe, 2000; Wiggins and McTighe, 2006).

A. Stimulating connections through analogy: "A big breath feels like you're really full, like your pants are too tight at the waist."

B. Stimulating connections through direct experience: Each summer, Mr. Tyler takes his freshman marching band members to a drum corps rehearsal the week before band camp. His students observe everything from fundamentals to full-corps practice sessions.

C. Stimulating connections through personal experience: Mrs. Zimmerman begins a discussion on the underpinnings of an "in memoriam" composition with the following questions:

- Have you ever been a victim?
- What does it mean to be a victim?
- Do we have to be victims?
- What can people do when they can't change their circumstances?

D. Stimulating connections through prior experience:

- "Let's say the B♭ scale alphabet."
- "How do we know which notes are sharp or flat?"
- "Let's do the same thing starting on E♭."

VI

I CAN'T TALK TO NOBODY, BABY

I HAVE TO KEEP IT ALL TO MYSELF

OH, I CAN'T TALK, I CAN'T TALK TO NOBODY, BABY

I HAVE TO KEEP IT ALL TO MYSELF

B.B. KING • "STOP PUTTING THE HURT ON ME"

SONGWRITER: RILEY KING

It's no secret. Homework is a four-letter word in the minds of many learners. Perhaps this is due to the all-too-frequent practice of assigning homework in which students must learn something new (e.g., performing in a new key or meter, or describing music of an unfamiliar genre). In contrast, homework *is* an effective strategy when the work to be done beyond the bells mirrors the work that is presently occurring between the bells. This type of practice helps the learners "internalize" skill and is central to developing flexible performance capacity.

> When skills are internalized, we don't have to pay attention to them and, thus, we can devote more attention to processing new information (Marzano, 1992, p. 61). In general, the more accuracy and speed with which a skill or procedure can be performed, the freer learners are to devote limited capacity of short-term memory to dealing with other issues, thus increasing the flexibility of their performance. (Marzano, 1992, p. 65)

A. Specific homework assignments that mirror instruction:

- "Practice this scale with the alternative fingering sequence we learned today."
- "Apply the rules of Italian grammar that we used in rehearsal today to this new song."
- "Practice these scales in legato style."
- "Your assignment is to format this score like we did in class today."
- "Apply the same process we used today to create a melody that conveys sadness."
- "Now it's your turn to try this on your own. Compose lyrics that flow from the sentence on the board."
- "Sight-read all of the exercises that are in the key of D♭ major."
- "Write the counts under the rhythms using the same system we used to count them verbally."

B. General homework assignment that mirrors instruction (not as effective, but important nonetheless):

- "Practice on the days you eat." (Greene, 1996, p. 15)

158

VII

BUFFALO ROY, WHAT'S YOUR TWENTY?

WHERE ARE YOU ANYWAY, BUFFALO ROY?

ARE YOU OUT THERE?

COME ON, ERE, BUFFALO ROY. 10-4.

C.W. MCCALL, BILL FRIES, CHIP DAVIS • "RATCHETJAW"

Running parallel to "instructional input" (or "teacher output") is the process of confirming whether or not ideas or information have been successfully received.

> *Formative* assessments occur concurrently with instruction. These ongoing assessments provide specific feedback to teachers and students for the purpose of guiding teaching to improve learning. (McTighe and O'Connor, 2005, p. 12)

In all episodes of instruction, the ultimate goal is not merely conveying ideas or information, but rather successfully conveying ideas or information—getting through. Thus, *confirmation shapes instruction*. Simply because something makes sense to someone who is older, wiser, and more experienced (a teacher), there is no reason to assume that it will automatically make sense to a student. Regardless of the instructional strategy employed, confirming whether or not students are actually "getting it" must be an ever-present counterpart. As Maxwell (1998) quips, "He who thinks he leads, but has no followers, is only taking a walk" (p. 20).

The reverse is also true: *instruction shapes confirmation*. Verifying the degree to which information has been absorbed, skills have been refined, etc., can be accomplished through a variety of formal and informal techniques. As with so many tasks, the right tool for the job makes everything easier.

159

A. *Checks for understanding* (note the absence of bobbing heads):

Fundamental Skills	Sight-reading
Artistry: Individual	Self-recordings
Artistry: Ensemble	Short performances by sections (i.e., low brass, cellos, sopranos) Recordings
Accuracy, Intonation	Short performances by a duet or trio of students
Concept Attainment	*Jeopardy*-style queries in which the teacher provides the answer and the students supply the question.
	Summary Game: The teacher asks, "What's the most important idea we've talked about today?" In reply, students record their answer(s) on a note card. After allowing adequate response time, students then pass the cards from desk to desk (in a frenzy!) until time is called. Each student then reads the idea on the card he or she ended up with and awards a score from 1–7 (7 is a great idea). After 5 rounds, the scores are tallied and a countdown from 35 to 1 begins. The winners are not the players, but the highest scoring ideas. (Thiagarajan, 2001)
	Brief summary sessions in which students are asked to list one word they think best describes the composition, concept, new idea, etc. Afterwards, the task is to turn the page over and write a paragraph that justifies their word choice. (Angelo, 1991)

VIII

THE LINE, IT IS DRAWN, THE CURSE, IT IS CAST

THE SLOW ONE NOW WILL LATER BE FAST

AS THE PRESENT NOW WILL LATER BE PAST

BOB DYLAN • "THE TIMES THEY ARE A-CHANGIN'"

What if, despite all the hours spent planning, preparing, teaching, and re-teaching, a student still doesn't "get it"? What if, despite all the hours spent planning and preparing, a student already "gets it"? A frequent outcome of attempting to teach anything to any group of learners is the need for intervention. Even after multiple attempts to reach all learners, rare is the occasion when all learners actually learn. According to Jenson (1998), each learner's brain is "a three-pound operating system…rich with intricate neural wiring that represents information, complex patterns, mental models, and belief systems" (pp. 41–42). Students bring their personal neural history to school each day, and teachers are given the challenge of customizing information for each learner. Ironically, Sylwester reminds us that in many classrooms "students are adapting to the teacher rather than the teacher adapting to them" (as cited in D'Arcangelo, 1998, p. 24).

In response to inexorable diversity among learners, the teacher action of merging confirmation—Johnny doesn't get it, Jessica already has it—with activity tailored to individual learner need(s) is arguably the only worthy defense against barriers to growth and achievement. The keyword, once again, is *action*. Every success story in education can be attributed to a teacher who was willing to give extra time or support to students who needed it. Regardless of tactic, when teachers initiate action, as opposed to thinking about taking action or wishing to take action, the potential for reversal is set in motion. As Benjamin Franklin reminds us, "Energy and persistence alter all things." Indeed, it's not so much that teachers don't know what to do, it's that teachers don't do. Perhaps the most common missing link in the instructional sequence is intentionally and consistently responding to the inevitable yet often tacit cries for another option. This is unfortunate, as effective intervention is just a wise decision away. For example:

- Kyle lives in a studio apartment with his mother and two sisters. Each night, he attempts to practice but is quickly admonished by his siblings. Kyle rarely reaches practice time requirements and scores poorly on weekly performance/chair tests.

  Intervention: Kyle's teacher hosts before- and after-school practice hours. He also makes the necessary arrangements for students who remain after school to catch a ride home on the athletic activity bus.

- Sarah lives in a two-story house with her sisters and parents. Each night, she practices in a spare bedroom upstairs. The room is far from the family room, so the rest of the household is generally undisturbed. Sarah always fulfills practice time requirements but scores poorly on weekly performance/chair tests.

  Intervention: Sarah's teacher intervenes by scheduling and delivering one-on-one tutoring sessions that are focused on "how to practice."

- The trombone section in Ms. Kappler's 8th grade band class is weak to say the least. In an act that surprised even the students themselves, Ms. Kappler programmed a song that featured the trombones (front and center) for the first concert of the year.

  Intervention: Ms. Kappler intervenes by putting into practice the fact that a weakness is never overcome by hiding it. As Booker T. Washington proclaims, "Few things help an individual more than to place responsibility upon him and to let him know that you trust him."

- Students in Mr. Able's orchestra class are given a calendar of optional music-making experiences on the first day of school. The schedule includes: (1) solo and ensemble events; (2) honor groups; (3) master classes; (4) peer tutoring; (5) concerto competitions; and (6) summer camps. Mr. Able also schedules weekly opportunities for students to perform audition music, solos, duets, etc., for the class.

Intervention: Mr. Able intervenes early by channeling the energy of those who want to make "more music more often" toward supplementary, yet very authentic, music-making experiences — curricular enhancements.

- Michael, a "squirrelly" freshman by all accounts yet a gifted trumpet player, finds himself frequently in detention as a result of attention seeking disguised in the form of rehearsal interruptions.

  Intervention: Upon his return, Michael's teacher intervened by moving his seat to the far left chair in the section, which was (cleverly) right next to the "hottest" senior girl in the band. Not surprisingly, the counterpart to attention — looking good — helps to keep Michael's behavior in check.

- Students in Mrs. Lampkin's sixth grade exploratory music classes are frequently given time to split into groups to obtain peer input about their work in relation to the project(s) at hand. Mrs. Lampkin strategically creates groups that each include fast learners, slow learners, and students at all points in between. Each assignment (performance) must be reviewed and signed by at least three peers before submission.

  Intervention: In Mrs. Lampkin's classes, "show your work to three of your peers before you show it to me" is a means of intervention. She knows that several of her students will need help with their assignments and that all students take something valuable from opportunities in which they assume the role of teacher.

IX

WHEN THE STORMS OF THE DAY HAVE ALL BLOWN AWAY
ALONG WITH FAIR WEATHER FRIENDS
THERE'S A PLACE I CAN GO WHERE THE WIND DOESN'T BLOW
IT'S THE BEST PLACE I'VE EVER BEEN

VINCE GILL • "SIGHT FOR SORE EYES"
SONGWRITERS: GUY CLARK, VINCE GILL

Physical surroundings influence behavior; people behave, act, or respond differently in different places. Additionally, many environments come with unique "behavior codes" that are often unspoken, but very real. For example, how do you feel (and act) when you enter one of the following places?

- Library
- Church
- Hospital
- Home that is in disarray
- Home that is orderly
- Movie theater
- Museum
- Restaurant
- Ballpark
- Gymnasium

In view of this reality, it is important to make the classroom an inviting place that encourages the kinds of behavioral and academic thoughts and actions teachers want students to demonstrate. Following are some ideas to stimulate the imagination:

A. *Décor with artistic overtones:*

- Framed pictures of famous musical artists
- Framed reproductions of famous paintings, drawings, etc.
- The Green Wall – autographs of prominent musicians and artists who have visited the classroom.

B. *Bulletin boards:*

- *Looking for more music in your life? Look here!* Fill the board with information on private lessons, summer camps, upcoming concerts, master classes, recitals, etc.
- *Sweet Success* (candy-themed board to highlight student achievement)
- *My Favorite Things* ("get to know the teacher" board)
- *Words of Wisdom* (message board from current students to future classes)
- *Above and Beyond* (permanent picture displays of students who have made exemplary contributions to the class or program)

> Have you ever entered a music room and noticed trophies and plaques that were broken, randomly placed, and entombed in dust? What does this say about the value of the accomplishments these items represent?

C. *Environmental factors:*

- How will time of day, grouping, posture, mobility, sound, lighting, and temperature influence the learners in your classroom?

X

I'D LIKE TO TEACH THE WORLD TO SING

IN PERFECT HARMONY

THE NEW SEEKERS • "I'D LIKE TO TEACH THE WORLD TO SING"
SONGWRITERS: ROGER COOK, BILLY DAVIS, ROGER GREENAWAY

Teaching is not for the weak. It never has been.

> Children today are tyrants. They contradict their parents, gobble their food, and tyrannize their teachers. (Socrates, c. 469–399 BC)

Teaching is for the strong. It always has been.

165

> Based on analysis of 50 years of educational research, of the 28 factors evaluated, classroom management had the greatest effect on school achievement. Working from a database of 11,000 findings, [Wang, Haertel, and Walbert] concluded that classroom management affected learning more than factors such as home environment, cognitive processes, school climate, school policies, and parental support. (Di Giulio, 2000, p. 5)

Unfortunately, whenever two or more humans are brought together, the results can range from absolute harmony to sheer dissonance.

> I have come to a frightening conclusion. I am the decisive element in the classroom. It is my personal approach that creates the climate. It is my daily mood that makes the weather. (Ginott, 1972/1994, pp. 15–16)

Clarence Francis succinctly illuminates this reality: "It seems abundantly clear that every problem you will have—in your family, in your business, in our nation, or in this world—is essentially a matter of relationships, of interdependence." Fortunately, *student* behaviors that lead to prime educational climates—in a classroom, on a football field, or on a stage—can be taught when *teacher* behaviors that lead to prime educational climates are learned. To this end, Di Giulio (2000) presents a framework for conceptualizing, organizing, and reflecting on interrelated practices that are central to peaceful and productive environments.

A Comprehensive Approach to Climate Control

	Physical Dimension	Instructional Dimension	Managerial Dimension
Preventive Intervention	*True or False?* The environment selects who we are and what we do. *True or False?* I can list several ways in which my classroom is conducive to prosocial behavior.	*True or False?* I am always prepared for class when students arrive. *True or False?* Students are always on task in my classroom; students have little opportunity to misbehave.	*True or False?* Well-rehearsed classroom operating procedures are in place in my classroom. *True or False?* My students know when, where, and how to ask for help. *True or False?* My students know what to do when they arrive at my classroom. *True or False?* My students know what to do if their instrument breaks during rehearsal. *True or False?* My students know where to put their backpacks. *True or False?* My students know when and where to turn in homework. *True or False?* All of my students help to create our classroom rules; "an idea shared becomes a movement toward inevitable progress" (Flaum, 2003, p. 7). *True or False?* My students know how I prefer to be addressed. *True or False?* My students know each other's names and how they prefer to be addressed. *True or False?* My students know what to do if an absence is inevitable.
Supportive Intervention	*True or False?* The seating configurations in my classroom allow me to quickly and easily get students' attention. *True or False?* My classroom can be described as a warm, inviting, and inspiring environment for learning.	*True or False?* Dynamic learning experiences are a daily occurrence in my classroom; I am continually working to improve my lessons and instruction; I know that "good enough" is the enemy of great. *True or False?* Learning is celebrated in my classroom. *True or False?* I teach students how to solve problems for themselves. *True or False?* I give my students frequent opportunities to share ideas for making the class more interesting; I ask my students how I can help them to become more successful.	*True or False?* The time to focus on behavior is not when things are going wrong, but rather when things are going right (M. Worthy, personal communication, June 4, 2004). *True or False?* I employ a variety of verbal and non-verbal reinforcements. *True or False?* I reinforce far more often than I enforce. *True or False?* Most of my attention is devoted to behaviors that I do want repeated in my classroom.

	Physical Dimension	*Instructional Dimension*	*Managerial Dimension*
Corrective Intervention	*True or False?* People are emotional first, rational second. *True or False?* Students who need a break or privacy have a place to go in my classroom.	*True or False?* I know how to address unacceptable behavior "in flight" and without a huge interruption to learning (e.g., proximity, circulation, verbal reminders, body language, eye contact, or practice time-outs). *True or False?* I do not allow people who cannot control their behavior to control mine; I bend but never break.	*True or False?* I respond to even the most undesirable behaviors in a professional manner. *True or False?* Reason precedes response in my classroom; I seek to understand before being understood. *True or False?* Consequences in my classroom are logical and practical; when correctives are required, I take time to determine an appropriate course of action; I do not make snap decisions in the heat of the moment. *True or False?* I deliver enforceable statements, not threats. *True or False?* I maintain comprehensive documentation of all discipline-oriented interactions. *True or False?* When necessary, I ensure the presence of a neutral witness when discussing or delivering correctives. *True or False?* I do not allow one student or a small group of students to consume all of my energy and attention. After repeated, comprehensive, and documented attempts to correct the situation, I employ the assistance of other professionals. I know that each of my students deserves my positive attention.

⇩
⇩

True or False?

If I had positive answers to each of these questions,

the great rehearsal techniques that I learned at the convention could really

be useful.

Creating a harmonious climate is not something to take lightly—there is much at stake for the learner, much more than meets the eye. In an environment where teacher and learners work in harmony to achieve meaningful goals, unspoken yet critical life messages (such as the following examples adapted from Tomlinson, 2002) have a fighting chance to pervade. In the words of Edgar Degas, "Art is not what you see, but what you make others see:"

168

I can handle the situations that life presents me.

People that I care about believe in me.

My ideas count.

I am respected.

I am trustworthy.

I am listened to.

I am needed.

I am accepted.

I am capable.

I can accomplish amazing things.

XI

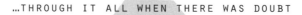

...THROUGH IT ALL WHEN THERE WAS DOUBT

I ATE IT UP AND SPIT IT OUT

I FACED IT ALL AND I STOOD TALL

AND DID IT MY WAY

FRANK SINATRA • "MY WAY"
SONGWRITERS: PAUL ANKA (ENGLISH), CLAUDE FRANCOIS, JACQUES REVAUX, GILLES THIBAUT

Of all the instructive actions in existence, perhaps the least effective is rejecting new ideas solely in defense of previous experience.

…think about what is needed for learning, not just what is comfortable for teaching. How much should we talk and how much should we let learners "do"? How much should we "cover" and how much should we help learners "uncover"?…The proportions are likely to be a ratio that you are not in the habit of using. (Wiggins and McTighe, 2006, p. 242)

As Michele Forman, 2001 National Teacher of the Year, proposes, "Learning is idiosyncratic. Learning and teaching is messy stuff. It doesn't fit into bubbles."

Précis

Brilliant teachers do not give students the opportunity, or at the very least minimize the potential opportunity, to make predictable mistakes, commit unacceptable behavior, squander their potential and, most importantly, fail. Such simple logic comes with such monumental implications.

TIME FALLS AWAY

BUT THESE SMALL HOURS

THESE LITTLE WONDERS

STILL REMAIN

ROB THOMAS • "LITTLE WONDERS"

As Mel Clayton, former national president of The National Association for Music Education, proposes, "Memories of a great teacher and of a quality music education will always provide our best means of getting support for music education." Keyword: *memorable*. With the help of a *guiding light*, students quickly become the beneficiaries of two wonderful things: an unforgettable experience and learning that lasts. This is the wonder and the reward of ***Destination: Illumination***.

QUESTIONS FOR REFLECTION

True or False?

I am a professional educator. I am expert at **adjusting** instructional strategies and materials in response to learner feedback and performance; **anticipating** problems; **assessing** as learning occurs; **assisting** fast learners, slow learners, and all students in between; **building** confidence; **celebrating** significant growth and achievement; **challenging** students to take risks; **clarifying** goals; **communicating** in a manner that encourages students to think for themselves; **connecting** lessons to life; **creating** the physical, psychological, emotional, and social conditions in which learning is most likely to occur; **delivering** constructive feedback; **demonstrating** artistic performance; **describing** transcendent musical moments; **directing** attention; **employing** instructional technology; **encouraging** risk-taking; **engaging** the mind; **focusing** attention; **guiding** learner practice; **highlighting** conventions and hallmarks of quality; **inspiring** effort; **improvising** under pressure; **intervening** as needed with correctives, enrichments, and specialized services; **leading** rehearsals and instructional episodes; **listening** with genuine interest; **matching** tactic to task or method to minds; **meeting** learner needs; **modeling** prosocial behaviors; **piquing** curiosity; **preventing** failure; **producing** artistic performances; **reminding** students of their strengths; **responding** to the moment; **sparking** attention; and **stimulating** active involvement.

Plot a potent path.

Light the way.

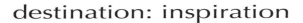

destination: inspiration

THE SECRET OF LIFE IS TO HAVE A TASK,
SOMETHING YOU DEVOTE YOUR ENTIRE LIFE TO,
SOMETHING YOU BRING EVERYTHING TO,
EVERY MINUTE OF THE DAY FOR THE REST OF YOUR LIFE.
AND THE MOST IMPORTANT THING IS,
IT MUST BE SOMETHING YOU CANNOT POSSIBLY DO.

—HENRY MOORE

When was the last time you had a sudden, brilliant idea? You know, the kind you can't wait to share. After applying this idea, did it have the impact you thought it would? Is it still producing desired results? Did it work well in a variety of contexts? If so, great! If not, welcome to a wretched reality of teaching. Need is never identical, and what works well in one situation is by no means guaranteed to work well in another. Thus, in many ways, exceptional educators are those who are able to inspire consequential growth and achievement in any type of weather. Of course, to inspire one must first be inspired, which brings the journey of **Inspiration** into focus: the never-ending quest for a better way. To be clear, we're not looking for just any good idea. This is a quest for ideas that glow with lasting value and consequence.

YOU LIVE, YOU LEARN

YOU LOVE, YOU LEARN

YOU CRY, YOU LEARN

YOU LOSE, YOU LEARN

ALANIS MORISSETTE • "YOU LEARN"
SONGWRITERS: GLEN BALLARD, ALANIS MORISSETTE

It only takes a spark to ignite a brilliant flame, and inspiration can stem from just about anything. Well-presented workshops, timely articles, and trusted mentors are good examples, but so are ocean waves, breakfast, and *reflection*. Accordingly, the questions to follow are presented for the express purpose of sparking thought and consideration. For organizational purposes, each "spark" is juxtaposed with an intersecting quality that is by and large an inarguable descriptor of an inspired educator. To get the full effect, read this chapter as quickly as possible. Just go with the first response that comes to mind. Based on trial runs, this should only take about nine minutes and forty-two seconds. Processing your answers, however, is entirely another story. That will take a lifetime.

al·tru·is·tic
adj **unselfish regard for or devotion to the welfare of others**
(*altruistic*, def. 1)

True or False?

As I give I get.

True or False?

Not everything that can be counted counts, and not everything that counts can be counted.

—ALBERT EINSTEIN

True or False?

Everyone is good at something.

Traina (as cited in Cruickshank and Haefele, 2001) explored the autobiographies of 125 prominent Americans to determine the qualities in teachers they valued. Topping the list was:

- subject-matter competence
- caring about students and their success
- distinctive character (virtuous qualities such as honest, decency, fairness, devotion, empathy, and selflessness)

> **cred·i·ble**
> *adj* **inspiring trust and confidence**
> (*credible*, def. 1)

True or False?

The following behaviors can compromise the credibility of even the most brilliant educators:

Arriving late

Leaving early

Talking smack about others

Dressing unprofessionally

Inferring to be the world's busiest person,

and therefore, deserving of special treatment

True or False?

Value must be demonstrated, not merely proclaimed.

Knight (2006) proposes that a teacher's credibility is determined in large part by student interpretations of learnable teacher behaviors. The Teacher Credibility Model includes:

- Competence (can explain complex material well, can "do" what you are teaching)

- Trustworthiness (such as following through on promises and treating all students equally)

- Dynamism (such as deviating to increase student interest and using a variety of teaching techniques)

> **en·thu·si·as·tic**
> *adj* filled with or marked by enthusiasm
> (*enthusiastic*, def. 1)

In *10 Traits of Highly Effective Teachers*, McEwan (2001) divides characteristics that lead to success in the classroom into three categories: (1) what an effective teacher is, (2) what an effective teacher does, and (3) what and how the effective teacher thinks. Central to what an effective teacher does is bringing drama, *enthusiasm*, liveliness, humor, charisma, creativity, and novelty to the classroom.

+

Sass (1989) reports that in surveys of more than twenty collegiate courses, students cite the same eight characteristics as major contributors to student motivation:

- Instructor's *enthusiasm*
- Relevance of the material
- Organization of the course
- Appropriate difficulty level of the material
- Active involvement of students
- Variety
- Rapport between teacher and students
- Use of appropriate, concrete, and understandable examples

=

True or False?
Enthusiasm is highly contagious…I should be a carrier.

In suggesting that teachers project enthusiasm we do not mean pep talks or unnecessary theatrics. Instead, we mean that *teachers identify their own reasons for viewing a topic as interesting, meaningful, or important and project these reasons to the students* when teaching about the topic (Good and Brophy, 2003, p. 238).

> **ex·em·pla·ry**
> *adj* so good or admirable that others would do well to copy it
> (*exemplary*, def. 1)

True or False?

Few things are harder to put up with than the annoyance
of a good example.

—Mark Twain

True or False?

Every child needs a hero.

True or False?

It could be me.

> **flex·i·ble**
> *adj* able to change or be changed according to circumstances
> (*flexible*, def. 1)

Kick (1992) offers paradoxical insight into the nature of teaching adolescents (p. 29):

- Don't hate the music I like.
- Don't like the music I like.
- Pay attention. If I act like something bugs me, that doesn't mean I don't like it.
- Pay attention. If I act like something doesn't bug me, that doesn't mean I do like it.
- Try to stay modern and with it.
- You'll never be able to be modern and with it.
- Ignore my moods.

- Pay attention to me when I tell you my feelings.
- Don't help me.
- Help me.

True or False?

I should bend but never break.

> **fo·cused**
> *adj* **concentrated on a single thing**
> (*focused*, def. 1)

True or False?

The magic of the "aha" moment is something to be revered.

True or False?

Learning is the ultimate touchstone of effective teaching.

> **fun**
> *adj* **like the time before daddy takes the T-bird away**

True or False?

Given a choice between fun and work, nine out of ten people will choose fun. And there are more "fun alternatives" available today than the world has ever known. So if we, using just a serious mindset, try to compete against fun, we will lose, hands down. To survive in today's world, we need to make music[ian]-making fun. (Chung, 2001, p. 24)

True or False?

A little nonsense now and then is relished by the wisest men.

—WILLIE WONKA

> **in·sight·ful**
> *adj* **...capable of clear and subtle perceptions about a subject**
> (*insightful*, def. 1)

True or False?

Mandatory observations, evaluations, certification requirements, background checks, blood tests, and reflections are things that teachers should respect.

True or False?

The role of the teacher remains the highest calling of a free people. To the teacher, America entrusts her most precious resource, her children, and asks that they be prepared.

—Shirley Mount Hufstedler, former U.S. Secretary of Education

True or False?

Teachers should be grateful that continuous professional development is a mandatory requirement.

True or False?

In times of change, learners inherit the earth while the learned find themselves beautifully equipped to deal with a world that no longer exists.

—Eric Hoffer

True or False?

It's the day after Thanksgiving and the teachers down the hall are going to have a heyday because you haven't taken down your Halloween bulletin board.

True or False?

In addition to having a heyday, one of the teachers will win the bet.

True or False?

You can swim all day in the Sea of Knowledge and still come out completely dry. Most people do.

—Norman Juster

True or False?

You can never learn less, you can only learn more.

—R. BUCKMINSTER FULLER

178 Berryburgfieldville High School is home to Mr. Smith, a highly successful football coach. This is also the home of Mr. Johnson, a highly frustrated band director. Each year, Mr. Johnson becomes more and more perplexed about why he loses upperclassmen, gets virtually the same results, and fights the same flavor of "battles" with his students. One fine day in February, Mr. Smith and Mr. Johnson had a long conversation. It didn't take long for Mr. Johnson to realize that he might be missing the boat.

Mr. Smith's Team		*Mr. Johnson's Team*
Distinct goals, including winning a championship and setting team and personal records, fuel effort, unity, and commitment.	**True or False?** The goal makes the team.	Indistinct goals fuel haphazard effort, unity, and commitment.
The series/season includes contests for audiences of fans, parents, friends, cheerleaders, scouts, school officials, and media. The season concludes with play-offs or a championship series with rankings, standings, and audiences of fans, parents, friends, cheerleaders, scouts, school officials, and media.	**True or False?** The greater the potential return, the greater the potential investment.	Students perform at several marching band contests for an audience of parents and competing bands. Students present two concerts to an audience of parents, friends, and the administrator who "lost the toss." Students attend a spring concert contest for a rating of I–V from three judges in an empty auditorium. Students are encouraged to select their own solo, prepare it independently, and perform it at district solo/ensemble contest to an audience of one judge.

Mr. Smith's Team	True or False?	Mr. Johnson's Team
The season is 3 to 4 months long and includes 10 regular season games and play-offs (if applicable).	The key to keeping your balance is to know when you've lost it.	The season is 9 months long and includes 5 home football games, 5 away football games, 4 contests, a march-a-thon, 3 parades, a Christmas concert, 7 home basketball games, a winter concert, district contest, state contest, an out-of-town festival, a spring concert, and graduation.
The off-season is devoted to fundamentals—fitness, nutrition, strength, technique, strategy, etc.		There is no off-season; there is no time to systematically focus on fundamentals.
Participation is a privilege. Students who do not keep passing grades, notify the coach of inevitable absences in advance, communicate immediately about unexpected absences, or memorize the week's play book by the deadline do not play.	**True or False?** Behavior is a result of its consequences.	Students who demonstrate a pattern of tardiness, absence, and/or lack of effort are allowed to perform under the assumption performances will be diminished without everyone in place, even if such students are underprepared.
Students compete each week for places on the starting team.		Students compete for first chairs once per semester.
The team is recognized at a school-wide assembly.	**True or False?** Whatever gets attention gets repeated.	The band performs for those being recognized at the school-wide assembly.
Banquets, photo shoots, professionally produced programs with player info and pictures are standard fare.		Trophies from past and present are collecting dust in a corner of the band room.
Comprehensive statistics of player and team performance are maintained and publicized.		
Signs in the gym and trophy cases lining the hallways provide frequent reminders of achievement.		

> **per·fect**
> *adj* **as good as it is possible to be**
>
> (*perfect*, def. 1)

180   And now, a message from our sponsors:

Listen up! Accept nothing less than the best…from all of us.

We need you to expect more from us than we do from ourselves.

This may sound strange to you, but some of us don't have a clue about our potential. Nobody ever talks about that. What we do understand is that if you allow us to set the bar of expectations, we may set it too low. We may not tell you, but we need you to demand the very best from us. Most likely we will try very hard not to disappoint you.

Be careful though. If you talk about high expectations and then accept our inferior work, you confuse us. And when we are confused, we will not do our best work. You see, what you say (your audio) must be in sync with what you do (your video)! In other words, we need you to walk the talk.

Our definition of high expectations is simple: we want you, at all times, in all ways, to expect and accept nothing less than the best from us. Sometimes we may act like you are being unreasonable. Just remember, when we resist your efforts, whining and pouting along the way, do not compromise your standards or lower your expectations of us.

We know the path of least resistance will tempt you to sometimes give up on us, but please don't. Our futures depend on it. (*Listen Up!*, n.d.)

True or False?

Being perfect is about being able to look your friends, your family, your neighbors, your peers, your students, and yourself in the eye and know that you told the truth. And that truth is you did everything you could. There wasn't one more thing that you could have done.

—ADAPTED FROM THE SCREENPLAY TO "FRIDAY NIGHT LIGHTS," SCREENWRITER: DAVID AARON COHEN, UNIVERSAL STUDIOS, 2004

> **pre·pared**
> *adj* ready and able to cope with something, often something hard or bad
>
> (*prepared*, def. 1)

Amid the horror of the Virginia Tech massacre on April 16, 2007, Professor Liviu Librescu held the door of his classroom, Room 204, shut while the gunman attempted to enter it. Librescu was able to prevent the shooter from entering the classroom until most of his students escaped through the windows, but he died after being shot multiple times through the door. Only one student in his classroom died (Donovan, 2007).

True or False?

A crazymaker could conceivably invade my school.

True or False?

I should know precisely what to do if a crazymaker invades my school.

True or False?

A student could conceivably choke, have a seizure, or faint without warning.

True or False?

When traveling with students, there should always be someone skilled in CPR and first aid.

pro·fes·sion·al
adj having or showing the skill appropriate to a professional person; competent or skillful

(*professional*, def. 1)

Strong (2002) cites the following "red flags" that are characteristic of unprofessional teachers (pp. 87–88):

- Gives negative feedback routinely at meetings
- Displays unwillingness to contribute to the mission and vision of the school
- Refuses to meet with parents and guardians or colleagues outside of contract hours
- Resents or is threatened by other adults visiting the classroom
- Does the minimum required to maintain certification or emergency certification status
- Submits reports late
- Submits grades late
- Writes inaccurate or unclear reports
- Does not update grade book or it is inaccurate

True or False?

You moon the wrong person…and suddenly you're not "professional" anymore.

—JEFF FOXWORTHY

True or False?

If you can't describe what you're doing as a process, you don't know what you're doing.

—W. EDWARDS DEMING

True or False?

Essential 21st-century skills are just as applicable to teachers as they are to learners.

21st-Century Skills	*Parallel (Professional) Practices*
Using knowledge meaningfully	Designing coursework and instruction that epitomizes problems to solve rather than answers to remember
Communicating successfully	Using a variety of verbal and non-verbal modes of communication to not merely convey information, but rather to "get through"
Collaborating effectively	Incorporating cooperative learning into instruction and assignments Initiating learning partnerships Profiling learners at the beginning of each term/course Organizing learning or practice communities within the class or program Developing and maintaining (modeling) supportive and cooperative relationships within the educational "village"
Using technology proficiently	Using technology to enhance curriculum, instruction, and assessment Using technology to enhance personal productivity
Accomplishing quality results efficiently	Establishing clear, measurable objectives that develop and demonstrate knowledge with lasting value and consequence Ensuring seamless congruity among goals, instruction, and assessment Adapting services and instruction to meet real-time learner needs Recognizing effort Establishing and meeting deadlines
Adapting to change fluidly	Respecting change

21st-Century Skills	Parallel (Professional) Practices
Learning independently and strategically	Participating fully in school-sponsored professional development Establishing and achieving personal professional development goals
Contributing to family, school, and community positively	Providing a model of professional and altruistic behavior at all times Bringing the principal solutions rather than problems Volunteering to serve, e.g., as a mentor, committee member, curriculum writer, or club sponsor

pur·pose·ful
adj **having a useful purpose**
(*purposeful*, def. 1)

True or False?

In the absence of clearly defined goals we become strangely loyal to performing daily trivia until ultimately we become enslaved by it.

—ROBERT HEINLEIN

True or False?

If I had to ask two people to describe the ultimate impact of my teaching, Simon Cowell and Dr. Phil would probably come the closest to getting it right.

real
adj **genuine and original; honest or sincere**
(*real*, def. 1)

In support of creating a prime environment for learning, Glasser (1993) recommends that teachers look for opportunities to let students know:

21st-Century Skills	Parallel (Professional) Practices
Who you are, e.g.,	I am your ally and my greatest talent is helping to develop yours.
What you stand for, e.g.,	Surpassing expectations.
What you will ask them to do, e.g.,	I will ask you to: Complete assignments. Self-evaluate. Make improvements. Repeat.
What you will not ask them to do, e.g.,	I will not ask you to be anyone other than yourself.
What you will do for them, e.g.,	I will seek to understand before being understood.
What you will not do for them, e.g.,	I will not accept mediocrity. Failure is not an option.

True or False?

To be persuasive we must be believable; to be believable we must be credible; to be credible we must be real.

—EDWARD R. MURROW

Self-a·ware

adj conscious knowledge of one's own character, feelings, motives, and desires

(*self-aware*, def. 1)

SOMETIMES YOU NEED SOMEONE TO SEE YOURSELF CLEARER

THERE'S NO REFLECTION WHEN IT'S YOU INSIDE THE MIRROR

MEREDITH BROOKS • "SHINE"

SONGWRITERS: MEREDITH BROOKS, DAVID DARLING, SHELLY PELKEN,

According to Peter Drucker, "who was often called the world's most influential business guru and whose thinking transformed corporate management in the latter half of the 20th century" (Sullivan, 2005, p. B06), people fail because of what they will not give up, clinging to what has worked in the past, even after it has clearly stopped working. Identically, Maxwell (1998) proposes, "To go up, you have to give up" (p. 192). Translation: Many of our struggles are self-induced.

Have you ever caught yourself being judgmental because someone else's view doesn't line up with your experience? What if we gave up thinking we had all the answers, delayed judgment, and considered the fact that diversity is the one true thing we all have in common.

> YOU CAN CHANGE YOUR FRIENDS, YOUR PLACE IN LIFE
> YOU CAN CHANGE YOUR MIND
> WE CAN CHANGE THE THINGS WE SAY
> AND DO ANY TIME
>
> VAN HALEN • "CAN'T STOP LOVIN' YOU"
> SONGWRITERS: MICHAEL ANTHONY, SAMMY HAGAR,
> ALEX VAN HALEN, EDWARD VAN HALEN

Have you ever found yourself surrounded by people who contaminate your perspective through tactics such as gossip, cynicism, moodiness, passive resistance, and general negativity? What if we gave up interacting with toxic people altogether, accepting the fact that the only thing of value between you and an unhealthy person is distance?

Have you ever stressed over something that never came to pass? Perhaps Mark Twain is on to something when he says, "I am a very old man and have seen considerably many troubles…most of which never happened." What if we gave up obsessing about what might happen and redirected that energy to what *is* happening?

Have you ever felt inadequate? What if we gave up delaying action because of self-doubt? Thoughts of inadequacy are natural but powerless to perseverance. As Leonardo da Vinci proclaims, "The painter who has no doubts will achieve little."

Have you ever caught yourself trying to do everything by yourself? What if we gave up trying to be superhuman and realized that asking for help is a sign of strength, not of weakness?

True or False?

People succeed because they give up.

> **te·na·cious**
> *adj* persistent in maintaining, adhering to,
> or seeking something valued or desired
> (*tenacious*, def. 1)

True or False?

Life is full of obstacle illusions—success belongs to those who have the fervor to succeed.

True or False?

"Now" is the operative word. Everything you put in your way is just a method of putting off the hour when you could actually be doing your dream. You don't need endless time and perfect conditions. Do it now. Do it today. Do it for twenty minutes and watch your heart start beating.

—Barbara Sher

True or False?

People succeed because they don't give up.

All'alba vincerò! Vincerò! Vincerò!

⇕

At daybreak I shall win! I shall win! I shall win!

Giacomo Puccini • Translator: Jason Siegal
Nessun dorma from *Turandot*

Précis

True or False?

I respect the primacy of truth.

QUESTIONS FOR REFLECTION

- *Who* do I want to be?
- *What* do I want to know?
- *Why* do I do what I do?
- *How* do I plan to grow?

finale

I WILL REMEMBER YOU

WILL YOU REMEMBER ME?

SARAH MCLACHLAN • I WILL REMEMBER YOU
SONGWRITERS: SEAMUS EGAN, SARAH MCLACHLAN, DAVE MERENDA

"This sure is good lemonade…I think I'll have another cup," said Mr. Buck. Then with a smile of delight, a smile so big he could hardly speak, he somehow managed to ask, "Mary, do you remember when the students…?"

When *you* are sitting on your front porch, reflecting on your career, what kind of thoughts will pervade? Will they be of the students who echoed your decision to become a music educator? Will they be about the remarkable young musicians, long graduated, who still keep in touch? How about the indescribable pride in Sarah's eyes after a best-ever performance? How about the day-to-day routine of seeing one student after another accomplish things they couldn't do before they met you? Or how about the students whose lives made a complete turnaround after you introduced them to the thoughts of others, frozen in melody, which mirrored their own?

As many who have walked before you would no doubt agree, this is only scratching the surface of the potential rewards from a *career* in music education. But if this type of recollection intrigues you, there is some really good news: decisive, responsive, inventive, brilliant, and inspired music educators are neither born nor created by others…they evolve. The journey begins by figuring out how to keep students in their seats, how to manage the never-ending winds of challenge and change, and how not to take things so personally. Eventually, thoughts of bigger and brighter things (such as making your choir actually sound like it does in your head) begin to merge with survival skills. Then almost magically, solutions to obstacles that once seemed insurmountable become increasingly clear. Like spotting an object far in the distance that only becomes distinguishable as you move towards it, expertise is the result of continual forward motion—*the journey forward to the place you first began.* As you've surely heard by now, through arts involvement students learn many skills necessary to succeed in life, including problem solving and decision making, building self-confidence and self-discipline, the ability to imagine what might be and to accept responsibility for it, teamwork, the development of informed perception, and articulating a vision[1]—***Destinations***.

Best wishes for a memorable journey. Oh, and just so you know, good memories come in two forms: memories of the good things that happened to you, and memories of the good things that you did for others. Wait a minute. That's wrong. There's only one.

God bless!

190

---

1   The Music for All Foundation.

appendix A

In conjunction with broad outcomes, documents that set forth music standards often include "achievement standards," which are also known as "proficiency objectives," "grade-level expectations," or "course-level expectations." Regardless of label, each specifies *benchmarks of achievement* at select junctures in a program of study.

To bring further clarity to these benchmarks—to look under the hood of musicianship—the following tables present data derived through analysis of achievement standards from across the United States. The publications included in the analysis are as follows:

Arizona Department of Education. (2006). *Arizona Music Standards.*

Delaware Department of Education. (2007). *Delaware recommended curriculum for music.*

Indiana Department of Education. (2007). *Indiana academic standards for music.*

Kendall, J. S., & Marzano, R. J. (2004). *Content knowledge: A compendium of standards and benchmarks for K–12 education.* Aurora, CO: Mid-continent Research for Education and Learning.

> *The Mid-continent Research for Education and Learning (McREL) Compendium synthesizes information from multiple documents, reports, and other materials compiled by professional education organizations. Specific to music, these resources include:*

Consortium of National Arts Education Associations. (1994). *National standards for arts education: What every young American should know and be able to do in the arts.* Reston, VA: MENC.

192

Visual and performing arts content standards for California public schools: Prekindergarten through grade twelve. (2001, January). California Department of Education.

The school music program: Description and standards. (1986). Reston, VA: MENC.

1997 arts education assessment framework. (1997). Washington, DC: National Assessment Governing Board.

MENC. (1994). *The school music program: A new vision. The K–12 national standards, pre-K standards, and what they mean to music educators.* Reston, VA: Music Educators National Conference.

In addition to the year of publication, these standards were selected because of common organizational characteristics, particularly complete or nearly complete alignment with the National Content Standards. In each of these publications, achievement standards associated with a particular National Content Standard were analyzed for content in three categories: (1) verbs, (2) objects, and (3) descriptors. For example, Indiana Standard 4.4.1, "Compose a melody for a verse of a selected poem and notate it using traditional or electronic means." (Indiana Department of Education, 2007, p. 20), was recorded as follows:

Verb	Object	Descriptor 1	Descriptor 2
composing	a melody	for a verse of a selected poem	
notating	a melody	for a verse of a selected poem	using traditional or electronic means

In the following tables, the total number of identical or similar verb, object, and/or descriptor combinations are presented in descending order. Only groups that occur in three or more publications are presented. This is not to discount the quality or importance of other standards but rather to illustrate *consensus*.

It is also important to note that publications included in this analysis present standards at varying levels:

- Standards in the MENC (1994) publication are presented at K–4, 5–8, and 9–12 grade levels.
- Standards in the McREL (2004) publication are presented at K–2, 3–5, 6–8, and 9–12 grade levels.
- Standards in the Delaware (2007) publication are presented for each grade level (K–12).
- Standards in the Arizona (2006) publication are presented for general music classes in grades K–8 and for specific performance-based courses in grades 9–12.
- Standards in the Indiana (2007) publication are presented for general music classes in grades K–6 and for specific music courses in grades 6–12.

Accordingly, the data in each table represents the following grade levels:

	EL (Elementary)	MS (Middle School)	HS (High School)
MENC (1994)	K–4	5–8	9–12
McREL (2004)	K–5	6–8	9–12
Delaware (2005)	K–4	5–8	9–12
Arizona (2006)	K–4	5–8	9–12
Indiana (2007)	K–4	5–8	9–12

Table 1:
Achievement Standards Associated with "Performing Music" (Verb + Object) that Occur in Three or More Publications

Verb	Object	Publications	Occurrences			
			EL	MS	HS	Total
playing	instruments	5	18	39	9	66
singing or playing	music at an appropriate or specific level of difficulty	4	0	7	51	58
responding to or following	the cues of a conductor	5	20	23	13	56
singing or playing	independent parts (within an ensemble)	5	7	15	31	53
singing or playing	a varied repertoire	5	3	16	24	43
playing	melodic patterns	5	8	21	11	40
singing or playing	repertoire in a variety of genres and styles	5	4	15	15	34
singing or playing	music written in two or more parts	5	2	13	12	27
singing or playing	rhythmic patterns	4	5	7	15	27
singing	unaccompanied music	5	4	9	9	22
singing	accompanied music	5	4	9	9	22
echoing, matching, or imitating	rhythmic patterns melodic, or harmonic patterns	5	13	5	1	19
singing or playing	accompaniments	4	2	14	3	19
playing	harmonic patterns; harmonic progressions	3	4	11	3	18
singing or playing	ostinatos	5	12	4	1	17
singing	rounds	5	6	6	1	13
singing	music in different languages	3	3	4	6	13
singing	partner songs	5	5	6	1	12

Sources
Arizona (2006): Strand 1: Create, Concept 1: Singing, alone and with others, music from various genres and diverse cultures; Strand 1: Create, Concept 2: Playing instruments, alone and with others, music from various genres and diverse cultures.
Delaware (2007): Standard 1: Singing independently and with others, a varied repertoire of music; Standard 2: Performing on instruments, independently and with others, a varied repertoire of music.
Indiana (2007): Standard 1: Performing Music: Singing alone and with others; Standard 2: Performing Music: Playing an instrument alone and with others.
McREL (2004): Standard 1: Sings, alone and with others, a varied repertoire of music; Standard 2: Performs on instruments, alone and with others, a varied repertoire of music.
MENC (1994): Standard 1: Singing, alone and with others, a varied repertoire of music; Standard 2: Performing on instruments, alone and with others, a varied repertoire of music.

Table 2:
Achievement Standards Associated with "Performing Music" (Verb + Descriptor) that Occur in Three or More Publications

Verb	Descriptor	Publications	Occurrences			
			EL	MS	HS	Total
Singing or playing…	…expressively	5	11	34	21	66
	…with appropriate intonation	5	15	25	26	66
	…with others; in an ensemble	5	18	32	15	65
	…with appropriate dynamics	5	19	25	20	64
	…with technical accuracy (vocal)	5	7	23	24	54
	…with technical accuracy (instrumental)	5	7	29	17	53
	…with appropriate posture	5	8	20	19	47
	…with appropriate phrasing	5	7	16	21	44
	…with characteristic tone quality	4	12	17	15	44
	…with accurate rhythm	5	11	16	11	38
	…with proper breath support	5	3	20	13	36
	…independently; alone	3	8	26	2	36
	…with a steady beat	5	18	2	12	32
	…from memory	4	6	10	11	27
	…with appropriate blend	5	6	6	11	23
	…with appropriate balance	4	1	7	12	20
	…accurately	4	4	5	10	19
	…with well-developed ensemble skills	4	3	0	12	15
	…with stylistic accuracy	3	2	9	3	14
	…by ear	3	2	7	2	11
	…with sensitivity to performance practices	3	0	10	0	10
	…with appropriate interpretation	3	2	2	2	6

Sources

Arizona (2006): Strand 1: Create, Concept 1: Singing, alone and with others, music from various genres and diverse cultures; Strand 1: Create, Concept 2: Playing instruments, alone and with others, music from various genres and diverse cultures.

Delaware (2007): Standard 1: Singing independently and with others, a varied repertoire of music; Standard 2: Performing on instruments, independently and with others, a varied repertoire of music.

Indiana (2007): Standard 1: Performing Music: Singing alone and with others; Standard 2: Performing Music: Playing an instrument alone and with others.

McREL (2004): Standard 1: Sings, alone and with others, a varied repertoire of music; Standard 2: Performs on instruments, alone and with others, a varied repertoire of music.

MENC (1994): Standard 1: Singing, alone and with others, a varied repertoire of music; Standard 2: Performing on instruments, alone and with others, a varied repertoire of music.

Table 3:
Achievement Standards Associated with "Improvising Music" that Occur in Three or More Publications

Verb	Object	Descriptor	Pub.	Occurrences			
				EL	MS	HS	Total
improvising	melodies		5	8	39	37	84
improvising	answers or responses to a musical prompt		4	20	2	0	22
improvising	solos or melodies	over chord progressions	5	0	6	15	21
improvising	harmonic accompaniments		5	0	10	10	20
improvising	harmonization, melodic embellishments, short ostinatos, variations, harmonic variations, melodic variations, or rhythmic variations	to familiar songs; to a familiar song; on familiar melodies; to a familiar melody; of a familiar melody; of a familiar song	4	9	6	5	20
improvising	rhythmic variations		4	3	7	9	19
improvising	melodic variations		4	2	5	9	16
improvising	rhythmic or melodic ostinato accompaniments		4	13	1	1	15
improvising	melodic embellishments		4	3	4	4	11
Sources							

Arizona (2006): Strand 1: Create, Concept 3: Improvising rhythms, melodies, variations, and accompaniments.
Delaware (2007): Standard 3: Improvising melodies, variations, and accompaniments.
Indiana (2007): Standard 3: Creating Music: Improvising melodies, variations, and accompaniments.
McREL (2004): Standard 3: Improvises melodies, variations, and accompaniments.
MENC (1994): Standard 3: Improvising melodies, variations, and accompaniments.

Table 4:
Achievement Standards Associated with "Composing and Arranging Music" that Occur in Three or More Publications

Verb	Object	Descriptor	Pub.	Occurrences			
				EL	MS	HS	Total
arranging, composing, or creating	[music]	according to teacher guidelines; under established guidelines; using teacher specified guidelines; with teacher guidance; within established guidelines; within specific guidelines; within specified guidelines; within teacher guidelines; within teacher specified guidelines	4	24	25	13	62
arranging	[pieces] instrumental pieces; short instrumental pieces; simple instrumental pieces; short sound pieces; vocal pieces; simple vocal pieces		4	8	9	5	22
composing or creating	[pieces] short instrumental pieces; short pieces		4	10	9	1	20
arranging, composing, or creating	[music]	with a variety of traditional and electronically produced sounds; with a variety of traditional sound sources; with a variety of sound sources; with a variety of nontraditional sound sources; using various pitched, non-pitched, and electronic sound sources; using a variety of traditional and non-traditional sound sources and electronic media; using a variety of sound sources; using a variety of acoustic or electronic sounds; choosing from a variety of sound sources	5	13	5	1	19

Table 4 (cont.)

Verb	Object	Descriptor	Pub.	Occurrences			
				EL	MS	HS	Total
notating	[music]	with compositional technology; using electronic means; using technology; using software; using notation software;	3	5	9	5	19
composing, or creating	[songs] songs; short songs		5	10	5	2	17
creating or writing	[compositions] compositions; combined vocal and instrumental compositions; complete compositions; original compositions; short compositions; short compositions for a specific instrument; short compositions for duet or small ensemble; sound compositions		3	2	4	11	17
composing or creating	[music] music; music for voices; music for various acoustic instruments; music for various electronic instruments		4	5	0	11	16
arranging, composing, or creating	[music]	to enhance a poem or short story; to accompany readings or dramatizations; to accompany or tell a story; to accompany an original descriptive text; to accompany a poem; for given texts; for a verse of a selected poem	4	9	7	0	16

Table 4 (cont.)

Verb	Object	Descriptor	Pub.	Occurrences			
				EL	MS	HS	Total
arranging	[music] music; music for voices; music for various acoustic instruments; music for various electronic instruments; piano music		4	3	0	9	12
Sources							
Arizona (2006): Strand 1: Create, Concept 4: Composing and arranging music. Delaware (2005): Standard 4: Composing and arranging music within specific guidelines. Indiana (2007): Standard 4: Creating Music: Composing and arranging music within specified guidelines. McREL (2004): Standard 4: Composes and arranges music within specified guidelines. MENC (1994): Standard 4: Composing and arranging music within specified guidelines.							

Table 5:
Achievement Standards Associated with "Reading and Notating Music" that Occur in Three or More Publications

Verb	Object	Descriptor	Pub.	Occurrences			
				EL	MS	HS	Total
[demonstrating]	music reading skills	through movement, singing, or playing instruments or body percussion.	5	23	51	75	149
defining, describing, distinguishing, explaining, identifying, knowing, recognizing, or understanding	standard musical symbols, terms, or notation		5	49	40	53	142
reading or following	standard or general musical symbols, terms, or notation		5	32	21	25	78
reading or decoding	rhythmic symbols, terms, or notation		5	29	14	21	64
notating	[music]	using standard notation symbols	5	16	23	21	60
reading, sight-reading, or following	vocal scores; instrumental scores; score symbols; symbols found in a musical score; traditional and non-traditional notation in musical scores; music symbols found in scores; expressive markings found in scores; simple musical scores		5	4	22	21	47
reading	[music]	at sight	5	2	13	13	28

Table 5 (cont.)

Verb	Object	Descriptor	Pub.	Occurrences			
				EL	MS	HS	Total
reading or sight-reading	melodies; melodic notation; melodic patterns; melodic lines		5	3	9	6	18
reading or sight-reading	(music)	in various major and minor key signatures; in major keys; in a variety of key signatures; in major and minor keys	3	2	7	6	15
	key signatures; music in specific keys						
Sources							
Arizona (2006): Strand 1: Create, Concept 4: Composing and arranging music. Delaware (2007): Standard 4: Composing and arranging music within specific guidelines. Indiana (2007): Standard 4: Creating Music: Composing and arranging music within specified guidelines. MENC (1994): Standard 4: Composing and arranging music within specified guidelines. McREL (2004): Standard 4: Composes and arranges music within specified guidelines.							

201

Table 6:
Achievement Standards Associated with "Analyzing and Describing Music" that Occur in Three or More Publications

Verb	Object	Pub.	Occurrences			
			EL	MS	HS	Total
analyzing, comparing, contrasting, describing, identifying, or recognizing	forms; musical forms	4	12	27	7	46
analyzing, comparing, describing, discussing, explaining, or identifying	elements of music	4	2	19	9	30
categorizing, classifying, describing, distinguishing, identifying, or naming	instruments	4	12	9	4	25
analyzing, classifying, comparing, contrasting, describing, expressing, or identifying	music representing various genres and/ or styles	4	2	12	10	24
classifying, comparing, describing, distinguishing, or identifying	voices; voice types; type of vocal ensemble	4	11	9	4	24
demonstrating, describing, or identifying	rhythmic elements, ideas, or values	3	6	15	0	21
using	musical terms	3	2	6	7	15
distinguishing, identifying, or recognizing	repetitions and contrasts; similar and contrasting sections; phrases as same or different	3	8	3	2	13
describing, explaining, or identifying	compositional devices and techniques	3	1	1	6	8
Sources						

Arizona (2006): Strand 3: Evaluate, Concept 1: Listening to, analyzing, and describing music.
Delaware (2007): Standard 6: Listen to, describing and analyzing music and musical performances.
Indiana (2007): Standard 6; Responding to Music: Listening to, analyzing, and describing music.
McREL (2004): n/a.
MENC (1994): Standard 6: Listening to, analyzing, and describing music.

Table 7:
Achievement Standards Associated with "Evaluating Music and Music Performances" that Occur in Three or More Publications

Verb	Object	Descriptor	Pub.	Occurrences			
				EL	MS	HS	Total
applying	criteria, specific criteria, or established criteria	when evaluating music or music performances	4	10	31	18	59
evaluating	music or music performances	by applying specific criteria					
offering	constructive suggestions for improvement	based on specific criteria					
creating, defining, developing, devising, establishing, evolving, identifying, or understanding	criteria for the evaluation of music and music performances; characteristics or qualities of effective music and music performances		5	8	25	21	54
using	appropriate terminology	within evaluations of music or music performances	5	10	10	11	31
identifying	musical characteristics	based on aural examples or listening	4	12	11	2	25
evaluating	music						

Table 7 (cont.)

Verb	Object	Descriptor	Pub.	Occurrences			
				EL	MS	HS	Total
analyzing, describing, discussing, evaluating, explaining, or identifying	characteristics;	that evoke a temperament or mood in a piece of music	4	I	I	6	8
	musical qualities	that evoke various responses or emotions in listeners and performers					
	relationships between music and human emotions						
	the musical means by which musical works evoke feelings and emotions						
Sources							
Arizona (2006): Strand 3: Evaluate, Concept 2: Evaluating music and music performances. Delaware (2007): Standard 7: Evaluating music and musical performances. Indiana (2007): Standard 7: Responding to Music: Evaluating music and music performances. McREL (2004): Standard 6: Knows and applies appropriate criteria to music and music performance. MENC (1994): Standard 7: Evaluating music and music performances.							

In addition to the data in Table 8, there were 65 standards (in 54 verb, object, and descriptor combinations) associated with classifying, comparing, contrasting, describing, discovering, distinguishing, explaining, exploring, identifying, recognizing, or tracing music from various genres, styles, cultures, and historical periods.

Table 8:
Achievement Standards Associated with "Relating Music" that Occur in Three or More Publications

Verb	Object	Pub.	Occurrences			
			EL	MS	HS	Total
analyzing, applying, classifying, comparing, considering, describing, discovering, discussing, experiencing, explaining, exploring, identifying, investigating, knowing, recognizing, or understanding	uses, roles, or functions of music	4	15	15	14	44
comparing, contrasting, creating, describing, discovering, discussing, explaining, exploring, expressing, identifying, mapping, recognizing	general interdisciplinary connections	4	7	15	9	31
citing, comparing, describing, discussing, exploring, identifying, knowing, recognizing, or understanding	roles or functions of musicians	5	13	8	9	30
analyzing, citing, comparing, describing, explaining, or identifying	connections among arts	3	3	4	10	17
citing, experiencing, exploring, identifying, knowing, recognizing, tracing, or understanding	genres of American music	4	1	2	8	11
explaining, identifying, or understanding	qualities or characteristics of exemplary music	3	1	6	1	8
Sources						

Arizona (2006): Strand 2: Relate, Concept 1: Understanding the relationships among music, the arts, and other disciplines outside the arts; Strand 2: Relate, Concept 2: Understanding music in relation to history and culture; Strand 2: Relate, Concept 3: Understanding music in relation to self and universal themes.

Delaware (2007): Standard 8: Making connections between music, the other arts, and other curricular areas; Standard 9: Understanding music in relation to diverse cultures, times, and places.

Indiana (2007): Standard 8: Responding to Music: Understanding relationships between music, the other arts, and disciplines outside the arts; Standard 9: Responding to Music: Understanding music in relation to history and culture.

McREL (2004): Standard 7: Understands the relationship between music and history and culture.

MENC (1994): Standard 8: Understanding relationships between music, the other arts, and disciplines outside the arts; Standard 9: Understanding music in relation to history and culture.

Table 9a:
Achievement Standards Associated with "Relating Music"
that Occur in Less than Three Publications
(sorted by number of occurrences)

Verb	Object	Descriptor	Pub.	Occurrences
exploring	the genre of repertoire being studied		1	8
exploring	the historical background of repertoire being studied		1	8
exploring	the style of repertoire being studied		1	8
describing	distinguishing characteristics of representative music genres	from various cultures; from a variety of cultures	2	4
describing	distinguishing characteristics of representative music styles	from various cultures; from a variety of cultures	2	4
describing	uses of the elements of music in various cultures; ways in which elements of music are used in music examples from various cultures of the world		2	4
exploring	music of other cultures; music of various world cultures	through live or recorded authentic performances	1	4
identifying	music from various genres; a varied repertoire of music from diverse genres		1	4
classifying	unfamiliar but representative aural examples of music; a varied body of exemplary musical works	by genre; by genre, explaining the reasoning behind classification choices	2	3
classifying	unfamiliar but representative aural examples of music; a varied body of exemplary musical works	by style; by style, explaining the reasoning behind classification choices	2	3
classifying	unfamiliar but representative aural examples of music; a varied body of exemplary musical works	by historical period; by historical period, explaining the reasoning behind classification choices	2	3
classifying	distinguishing characteristics of representative music genres	from various cultures	1	3
classifying	distinguishing characteristics of representative music genres	from various historical periods	1	3

Table 9a (cont.)

Verb	Object	Descriptor	Pub.	Occurrences
classifying	distinguishing characteristics of representative music styles	from various cultures	1	3
classifying	distinguishing characteristics of representative music styles	from various historical periods	1	3
comparing	a varied repertoire of music from diverse genres		1	3
comparing	a varied repertoire of music from diverse musical styles		1	3
describing	distinguishing characteristics of representative music genres	from various historical periods	1	3
describing	distinguishing characteristics of representative music styles	from various historical periods	1	3
describing	uses of the elements of music in various genres		1	3
describing	uses of the elements of music in various historical periods		1	3
describing	uses of the elements of music in various styles		1	3
identifying	a varied repertoire of music from diverse musical styles		1	3
classifying	unfamiliar but representative aural examples of music	by culture; by culture, explaining the reasoning behind classification choices	2	2
identifying	music from various cultures; aural examples from various cultures	by genre	2	2
identifying	music from various cultures; aural examples from various cultures	by style	2	2
identifying	music from various historical periods; aural examples of music from various historical periods	by genre	2	2
identifying	music from various historical periods; aural examples of music from various historical periods	by style	2	2
contrasting	music of various world cultures	through live or recorded authentic performances	1	2

Table 9b:
Achievement Standards Associated with "Relating Music" that Occur in Less than Three Publications

Verb	Object	Descriptor	Pub.	Occurrences
describing	characteristics that distinguish one historical period of music from another		1	2
describing	characteristics that distinguish one style of music from another		1	2
exploring	various musical genres of Europe and the Americas; various musical genres from Asia, Africa, Europe, and the Americas		1	2
exploring	various musical styles of Europe and the Americas; various musical styles from Asia, Africa, Europe, and the Americas		1	2
classifying	distinguishing characteristics of representative music genres	from a variety of cultures	1	1
classifying	distinguishing characteristics of representative music styles	from a variety of cultures	1	1
comparing	characteristics that distinguish one historical period of music from another		1	1
comparing	characteristics that distinguish one style of music from another		1	1
contrasting	characteristics that distinguish one historical period of music from another		1	1
contrasting	characteristics that distinguish one style of music from another		1	1
discovering	relationships between music from earlier periods in history and other elements in society		1	1
distinguishing	unfamiliar works of different cultures	based on aural identification of representative characteristics	1	1

Table 9b (cont.)

Verb	Object	Descriptor	Pub.	Occurrences
distinguishing	unfamiliar works of different genres	based on aural identification of representative characteristics	I	I
distinguishing	unfamiliar works of different historical periods	based on aural identification of representative characteristics	I	I
distinguishing	unfamiliar works of different styles	based on aural identification of representative characteristics	I	I
explaining	stylistic features of a given musical work that serve to define its aesthetic tradition and its historical or cultural context		I	I
identifying	music from diverse cultures		I	I
identifying	music genres that show the influence of two or more cultural traditions		I	I
identifying	cultural sources of music genres that show the influence of two or more cultural traditions		I	I
identifying	music styles that show the influence of two or more cultural traditions		I	I
identifying	cultural sources of music styles that show the influence of two or more cultural traditions		I	I
identifying	stylistic features of a given musical work that serve to define its aesthetic tradition and its historical or cultural context		I	I
recognizing	characteristics of music from various Western and non-Western cultures		I	I
tracing	historical conditions that produce synthesized influences on music genres being studied		I	I

Appendix B

Sample ICU (Intensive Care Unit)

	Accommodation (Strategy)					Concentration (Focus)
	Rehearsal-Level Objective/Assessment #1 — Week 2	Rehearsal-Level Objective/Assessment #2 — Week 3–4	Rehearsal-Level Objective/Assessment #3 — Weeks 4–6	Rehearsal-Level Objective/Assessment #4 — Weeks 6–7	Rehearsal-Level Objective/Assessment #5 — Week 8	Unit-Level Objective/Assessment
(AB + CD)	Select a topic associated with the concert music from the teacher-provided list. Create at least 5 open-ended questions about your topic. Turn in your questions for approval.	Locate at least 3 sources from the library and 3 sources from the Internet that provide answers to your questions.	Create a first draft by (a) combining information from your sources to answer each of your questions, (b) sequencing your answers to tell an interesting story, and (c) citing your sources correctly.	Ask 2 adults to proofread and sign your work. Use the feedback and teacher-provided rubric to revise your work. Turn in your original and revised drafts by the deadline.	Use your final draft to create a 1-minute presentation that summarizes important discoveries from your investigation. Give your presentation to the class on the assigned date.	Based on a select topic associated with the concert music, the students will create comprehensive notes for the program.

Evaluation (Hallmarks of Quality; Evaluative Criteria)

	#1 — Week 2	#2 — Week 3–4	#3 — Weeks 4–6	#4 — Weeks 6–7	#5 — Week 8	Unit-Level
(= E)	The students: ☐ chose a topic from the list. ☐ created 5 questions. ☐ submitted questions for approval.	The students: ☐ used reliable sources to answer his or her questions.	The draft: ☐ represents appropriate effort and progress. ☐ tells an interesting story. ☐ was proofread by 2 adults. ☐ includes information from reliable sources. ☐ is free of misspelled words and grammatical errors. ☐ includes correct citations of sources (3 library, 3 Internet).		The presentation was: ☐ 1 minute in length. ☐ a summary of important points. ☐ given on assigned date.	The program notes: ☐ present information clearly. ☐ present information that is accurate. ☐ present information that is interesting. ☐ are original (not plagiarized). ☐ are free of misspelled words and grammatical errors. ☐ include at least 3 correctly cited sources from the library. ☐ include at least 3 correctly cited sources from the Internet.

Reflection (Alignment with Local Priorities)

Artistic Perceptions > 1. Develop and apply the knowledge and skills to listen to, analyze, and describe music and musical performance > A. Musical Forms > 9–12: Identify forms used in selected ensemble repertoire

Artistic Perceptions > 1. Develop and apply the knowledge and skills to listen to, analyze, and describe music and musical performance > B. Musical Characteristics, Events, and Descriptors > 9–12: Characterize the use of music by its intended function (purpose) and its intended audience

Artistic Perceptions > 2. Develop and apply the knowledge and skills to evaluate music and musical performance > B. Critique Musical Performances and Compositions > 9–12: Use musical terminology to describe their personal response to musical example

Interdisciplinary Connections > 1. Develop and apply knowledge and skills to understand the relationships between music, the other arts and disciplines outside the arts > A. Connections Between Music and Related Arts and Humanities > 9–12: Explain how elements, artistic processes (such as imagination or skills), and organizational principles (such as unity and variety or repetition and contrast) are used in similar and distinctive ways in the various arts and cite examples

Historical and Cultural Contexts > 1. Develop and apply the knowledge and skills to understand works of art in time and place > A. Genres and Styles > 9–12: Identify music from various styles and historical periods by comparing and contrasting selected elements of music

Historical and Cultural Contexts > 1. Develop and apply the knowledge and skills to understand works of art in time and place > B. Stylistic Practices > 9–12: Describe the historical significance of selected music literature.

Historical and Cultural Contexts > 1. Develop and apply the knowledge and skills to understand works of art in time and place > C. Music's Role and Function in Various Cultures > 9–12: Categorize the function of music being performed in relation to its function in society or history.

	#1 — Week 2	#2 — Week 3–4	#3 — Weeks 4–6	#4 — Weeks 6–7	#5 — Week 8	Unit-Level
State GLEs/CLEs (Missouri Department of Elementary and Secondary Education, 2007)	1.1 develop questions and ideas to initiate and refine research	1.2 conduct research to answer questions and evaluate information and ideas; 1.4 use technological tools and other resources to locate, select, and organize information; 1.7 evaluate the accuracy of information and the reliability of its sources	1.6 discover and evaluate patterns and relationships in information, ideas, and structures; 1.8 organize data, information, and ideas into useful forms (including charts, graphs, outlines) for analysis or presentation	2.2 review and revise communications to improve accuracy and clarity	2.1 plan and make written, oral, and visual presentations for a variety of purposes and audiences	1.8 organize data, information, and ideas into useful forms (including charts, graphs, outlines) for analysis or presentation
State Process Standards (Missouri Department of Elementary and Secondary Education, 1996)						2.1 plan and make written, oral, and visual presentations for a variety of purposes and audiences

State Content Standards (Missouri Department of Elementary and Secondary Education, 1996)	FA 2 the principles and elements of different art forms FA 3 the vocabulary to explain perceptions about and evaluations of works in dance, music, theater, and visual arts FA 4 interrelationships of visual and performing arts and the relationships of the arts to other disciplines FA 5 visual and performing arts in historical and cultural contexts	CA 3 reading and evaluating nonfiction works and material (such as biographies, newspapers, technical manuals)	CA 1 speaking and writing standard English (including grammar, usage, punctuation, spelling, capitalization) CA 4 writing formally (such as reports, narratives, essays) and informally (such as outlines, notes)	CA 1 speaking and writing standard English (including grammar, usage, punctuation, spelling, capitalization) CA 4 writing formally (such as reports, narratives, essays) and informally (such as outlines, notes)	CA 6 participating in formal and informal presentations and discussions of issues and ideas	CA 1 speaking and writing standard English (including grammar, usage, punctuation, spelling, capitalization) CA 4 writing formally (such as reports, narratives, essays) and informally (such as outlines, notes) FA 2 the principles and elements of different art forms FA 3 the vocabulary to explain perceptions about and evaluations of works in dance, music, theater, and visual arts FA 4 interrelationships of visual and performing arts and the relationships of the arts to other disciplines FA 5 visual and performing arts in historical and cultural contexts
National Content Standards (MENC, 1994)	6. Listening to, analyzing, and describing music. 8. Understanding relationships between music, the other arts, and disciplines outside the arts. 9. Understanding music in relation to history and culture.					
Technology Standards (ISTE, 2007)	3. Students apply digital tools to gather, evaluate, and use information. Students: (b) locate, organize, evaluate, synthesize, and ethically use information from a variety of sources and media; (c) evaluate and select information sources and digital tools based on the appropriateness to specific tasks; (d) process data and report results. 4. Students use critical thinking skills to plan and conduct research, manage projects, solve problems, and make informed decisions using appropriate digital tools and resources. Students: (a) identify and define authentic problems and significant questions for investigation; (b) plan and manage activities to develop a solution or complete a project; (c) collect and analyze data to identify solutions and/or make informed decisions.					
Essential Questions	Who is this? Why is he or she important? What is this? Why is it important?					
Enduring Understandings	Beauty is in the eye of the educated beholder. Opinion and perspective are two different things. Art imitates life.					
Bloom's Taxonomy (Revised)	Analyze	Apply	Analyze; Create	Analyze; Evaluate	Analyze; Create	Create
21st Century Skills	Using knowledge meaningfully; communicating successfully; using technology proficiently; accomplishing quality results efficiently; learning independently and strategically					
Habits of Mind (Costa & Kallick)	Persisting; thinking and communicating with clarity and precision; striving for accuracy; questioning and posing problems					
Diversity-Related (Richards, Brown & Forde, 2006)	Educate students about the diversity of the world around them. Foster a positive interrelationship among students, their families, the community, and school. Motivate students to become active participants in their learning. Encourage students to think critically. Challenge students to strive for excellence as defined by their potential.					
Character-Related	Honesty					

bibliography

altruistic, def. 1. (2009). In *Merriam-Webster Online Dictionary*. Retrieved from http://www.merriam-webster.com/dictionary/altruistic

American School Band Directors Association. (1997). *The new ASBDA curriculum guide*. Miami, FL: Warner Brothers.

Anderson, J. R., Reder, L. M., & Simon, H. A. (2000, Summer). *Applications and Misapplications of Cognitive Psychology to Mathematics Education*. Texas Educational Review. Retrieved from http://act-r.psy.cmu.edu/papers/misapplied.html

Anderson, L. W. (2005). *Facilitators' guide for the taxonomy academy*. Columbia, SC: The Anderson Research Group. Retrieved from http://www.andersonresearchgroup.com/tax.html

Anderson, L. W. (2005). *Taxonomy academy handbook*. Columbia, SC: The Anderson Research Group. Retrieved from http://www.andersonresearchgroup.com/tax.html

Anderson, L. W. & Krathwohl, D. R. (Eds.). Airasian, P. W., Cruikshank, K. A., Mayer, R. E., Pintrich, P. R., Raths, J., & Wittrock, M. C. (Contributors). (2001). *A taxonomy for learning, teaching, and assessing: A revision of bloom's taxonomy of educational objectives* (complete edition). New York: Addison Wesley Longman.

Angelo, T. (1991). Ten easy pieces: Assessing higher learning in four dimensions. In T. Angelo (Ed.). *Classroom research: Early lessons from success: New dimensions for teaching and learning, no. 46*. San Francisco: Jossey-Bass.

Apfelstadt, H. (1989). Musical thinking in the choral rehearsal. In E. Boardman (Ed.). *Dimensions of musical thinking* (pp.73–81). Reston, VA: Music Educators National Conference.

Arizona Department of Education. (2006). *Arizona music standards*. Retrieved from http://www.ade.state.az.us/standards/arts/revised/Music.pdf

Armstrong, S. & Armstrong, S. (1996, May). The conductor as transformational leader. *Music Educators Journal 82*(6), 22–25.

Bacon, F. (1620). *Novum Organum* B. Montague (Ed. and Trans.). Retrieved from http://history.hanover.edu/texts/Bacon/novorg.html

Best, H. (1995). Musical perception and music education. *Arts Education Policy Review 96*(4), 2–9.

Billings, D. (2003). *Entitled to fail, endowed to succeed: America's journey back to greatness.* Bixby, OK: DCB Publishing.

Bixler, B. (2006). *Writing educational goals and objectives.* Retrieved from http://www.personal.psu.edu/staff/b/x/bxb11/Objectives/

Blakey, E. & Spence, S. (1990). *Developing metacognition.* Retrieved from ERIC database (ED327218). Available at http://www.ericdigests.org/pre-9218/developing.htm

Blatner, A. (2002). Role playing in education. Retrieved from http://www.blatner.com/adam/pdntbk/rlplayedu.htm

Boardman, E. (2001, September). Generating a theory of music instruction. *Music Educators Journal 88*(2), 45–53.

Boers, D. (2001). What I hope for in my children's teachers: One parent's perspective. *The Clearing House, 75*(1), 51–54.

Bolar, A. (2004). *Railroads: History through music* (lesson plan). Retrieved from http://coreknowledge.org/CK/resrcs/lessons/04_Mus2_Railroad.pdf

Bransford, J. D., Brown, A. L., & Cocking, R. R. (Eds.). (2000). *How people learn: Brain, mind, experience, and school* (expanded ed.). Washington, DC: National Academy Press.

Brooks, J. G. & Brooks, M. G. (1993). *The case for constructivist classrooms.* Alexandria, VA: Association for Supervision and Curriculum Development.

Bruner, J. (1960). *The process of education.* Cambridge, MA: Harvard University Press.

214

Business Wire. (2006, April 21). *Norlight expands IP telephony offerings in wisconsin; company uniquely positioned in marketplace.* Business Wire. Retrieved from http://www.allbusiness.com/media-telecommunications/5469616-1.html

California Department of Education. (2004). *Visual and performing arts framework for California public schools: Kindergarten through grade twelve.* Retrieved from http://www.cde.ca.gov/ci/cr/cf/documents/vpaframewrk.pdf

Cawelti, G. (1995). *Handbook of research on improving student achievement.* Arlington, VA: Educational Research Service.

Chappuis, S. & Stiggins, R. J. (2002, September). Classroom assessment for learning. *Educational Leadership 60*(1), 40–43.

Children's Defense Fund. (2008). Moments and each day in America for children. *The state of America's children: 2008.* Washington D.C.: Children's Defense Fund. Retrieved from http://www.childrensdefense.org/child-research-data-publications/data/state-of-americas-children-2008-report-moments-each-day.pdf

Chiodo, P. (2001). Assessing a cast of thousands. *Music Educators Journal 87*(6), 17-23.

Chung, B. (2001, November). Seeing the bigger picture. *School Band and Orchestra 4*(10), 21–26.

Clark, D. R. (2004). Instructional system design concept map. Retrieved from http://nwlink.com/~donclark/hrd/ahold/isd.html

coherent, def. 1 (2009). In *Cambridge Advanced Learner's Dictionary.* Retrieved from http://www.merriam-webster.com/dictionary/coherent

Colman, A.M. (2001). *A dictionary of psychology.* Oxford University Press. Retrieved from Encyclopedia.com website: http://www.encyclopedia.com/doc/1O87-declarativeknowledge.html

Colorado Department of Education. (1997, November). *Colorado model content standards for music.* Available at http://www.cde.state.co.us/cdeassess/documents/OSA/standards/music.htm

215

Comer, J. (2001, April 23). Schools that develop children. *The American Prospect 12*(7). Retrieved from the LexisNexis Academic database.

Consortium of National Arts Education Associations. (1994). *National standards for arts education*. Reston, VA: Music Educators National Conference. Retrieved from http://artsedge.kennedy-center.org/teach/standards/

core, def. 1. (2009). In *Encarta World English Dictionary* (North American edition). Retrieved from http://encarta.msn.com/dictionary_/core.html

Cosenza, G. (2005, September 8). Implications for music educators of an interdisciplinary curriculum. *International Journal of Education and the Arts 6*(9). Retrieved from http://www.ijea.org/v6n9/v6n9.pdf

Costa, A. L. & Kallick, B. (n.d.) What are habits of mind? Retrieved from habits-of-mind.net website: http://www.habits-of-mind.net/whatare.htm

credible, def. 1. (2009). In *Encarta World English Dictionary* (North American edition). Retrieved from http://encarta.msn.com/dictionary_/credible.html

Cruickshank, D. & Haefele, D. (2001). Good teachers, plural. *Educational Leadership 58*(5), 26–30.

Cummings, C. (2000). *Winning strategies for classroom management*. Alexandria, VA: Association for Supervision and Curriculum Development. Retrieved from http://www.ascd.org/publications/books/100052/chapters/Bonding_and_Connecting.aspx

Cunningham, P. M. & Allington, R. L. (2006). *Classrooms that work: They can all read and write* (4th ed.). San Francisco: Allyn and Bacon.

D'Arcangelo, M. (1998). The brains behind the brain. *Educational Leadership 56*(3), 20–25.

Delaware Department of Education. (2007). *Delaware recommended curriculum: Music*. Retrieved from http://www.doe.k12.de.us/infosuites/staff/ci/content_areas/files/vpa/MusicGLEPLE092007.pdf

Delpit, L. (2006). *Other people's children: Cultural conflict in the classroom* (updated ed.). New York: New Press.

DeRoche, D. (2002) Do not underestimate your students, as they deserve your very best. *Leblanc Bell 26*(1), 19–20.

Di Giulio, R. (2000). *Positive classroom management* (2nd ed.). Thousand Oaks, CA: Corwin Press.

District of Columbia Public Schools. (2008-2009). *DCPS teaching and learning framework resources overview*. Retrieved from http://dcps.dc.gov/ DCPS/Files/downloads/TEACHING%20&%20LEARNING/ Teaching-Learning-Framework/DCPS-Teaching-Learning-Framework-Binder-Resources-September-2009.pdf

Domjan, M. (2005). *The principles of learning and behavior* (5th ed.). Belmont, CA: Wadsworth.

Donovan, D. (2007, April 17). I don't think my teacher got out. *The Baltimore Sun*.

Donovan, M. S., Bransford, J. D., & Pellegrino, J. W. (Eds.). (1999). *How people learn: Bridging research and practice*. Washington, DC: National Academy Press.

Duke, R. A. (2005). *Intelligent music teaching: Essays on the core principles of effective instruction*. Austin, TX: Learning and Behavior Resources.

Duke, R. A. & Simmons, A. L. (2006). The nature of expertise: Narrative descriptions of 19 common elements observed in the lessons of three renowned artist-teachers. *Bulletin of the Council for Research in Music Education 170*, 1–13. Retrieved from http://www.cml.music. utexas.edu/DistinguishedStream/Abstract.htm

Dweck, C. (2000, April). How can teachers develop students' motivation—and success? *Education World 1*(1), 12–14.

Edwards, C. H. (1995). *A systematic approach to instructional design* (2nd ed.). Champaign, IL: Stipes.

Einstein, A. (1954, 1982). *Ideas and opinions*. New York: Three Rivers Press.

Elliot, D. J. (1995). *Music matters: A new philosophy of music education*. New York: Oxford University Press.

enthusiastic, def. 1. (2009). In *Merriam-Webster Online Dictionary*. Retrieved from http://www.merriam-webster.com/dictionary/enthusiastic

exemplary, def. 1. (2009). In *Encarta World English Dictionary* (North American edition). Retrieved http://encarta.msn.com/dictionary_/exemplary.html

expectation, def. 1. (2009). In *Encarta World English Dictionary* (North American edition). Retrieved from http://encarta.msn.com/dictionary_/expectation.html

expectation, def. 2. (n.d.). *Webster's Revised Unabridged Dictionary*. Retrieved from Dictionary.com website: http://dictionary1.classic.reference.com/browse/expectation

Flaum, S. (2003). When ideas lead; people follow. *Leader to Leader 30*, 7–12.

flexible, def. 1. (2009). In *Encarta World English Dictionary* (North American edition). Retrieved from http://encarta.msn.com/dictionary_/flexible.html

Florida State University. (n.d.). Retrieved from the College of Medicine Faculty Development website: http://med.fsu.edu/education/FacultyDevelopment/objectives.asp

focused, def. 1. (2009). In *Encarta World English Dictionary* (North American edition). Retrieved from http://encarta.msn.com/dictionary_/focused.html

Gaddy, B. B., Dean, C. B., & Kendal, J. S. (2002). *Noteworthy perspectives: Keeping the focus on learning*. Aurora, CO: Mid-continent Research for Education and Learning. Retrieved from http://www.mcrel.org/PDF/Noteworthy/5022IR_NW_Focus.pdf

Gardner, H. (1983). *Frames of mind: The theory of multiple intelligences*. New York: Basic Books.

Gatto, J. T. (1991). *The six-lesson schoolteacher*. Retrieved from Rocky Mountain Education Connection web site: http://www.rmec-online.com/articles/sixlesson.html

Gatto, J. T. (1995). *Personal solutions, family solutions*. Retrieved from http://www.naturallifemagazine.com/9510/gatto.htm

Ginott, H. (1994). *Teacher and child: A book for parents and teachers* (1972 reprint). New York: Simon & Schuster.

Glasgow, N. A. & Hicks, C. D. (2009). *What successful teachers do: 101 research-based classroom strategies for new and veteran teachers* (2nd ed.). Thousand Oaks, CA: Corwin.

Glasser, W. (1993). *The quality school teacher.* New York: HarperCollins.

goal, def. 1. (2001). In *The New Oxford American Dictionary* (2nd ed.). Oxford University Press. Retrieved from Oxford American Dictionaries [computer software].

Good, T. L. & Brophy, J. E. (2003). *Looking in classrooms* (9th ed.). Boston: Allyn & Bacon.

Greene, J. (1996). Practice can make perfect if students learn correct habits from the outset. *Leblanc Bell 19*(1), 15–16.

Guskey, T. R. & Schultz, T. (1996). *Implementing Mastery Learning* (2nd ed.). Belmont, CA: Wadsworth.

Hardiman, M. M. (2001, November). Connecting brain research with dimensions of learning. *Educational Leadership 59*(3), 52–55.

Heinich, R., Molenda, M., Russell, J. D. & Smaldino, S. E. (1996). *Instructional media and technologies for learning* (5th ed.). Englewood Cliffs, NJ: Prentice Hall.

Hinckley, J. M. (1999). Statement before the subcommittee on early childhood, youth and families of the house committee on education and the workforce. Retrieved from http://www.amc-music.com/musicmaking/policy/hinckley.htm

-ian, def. 1. (2001). In *The New Oxford American Dictionary* (2nd ed.). Oxford University Press. Retrieved from Oxford American Dictionaries [computer software].

-ian, def. 2 (2009). In *Merriam-Webster Online Dictionary*. Retrieved from http://www.merriam-webster.com/dictionary/-ian

Indiana Department of Education. (2007). *Indiana academic standards for music*. Retrieved from http://dc.doe.in.gov/Standards/AcademicStandards/PrintLibrary/docs-Arts/2007-10-04-INMusicStandards.pdf

insightful, def. 1. (2009). In *Encarta World English Dictionary* (North American edition). Retrieved from http://encarta.msn.com/dictionary_/insightful.html

invitation, def. 1. (2001). In *The New Oxford American Dictionary* (2nd ed.). Oxford University Press. Retrieved from Oxford American Dictionaries [computer software].

ISTE-International Society for Technology in Education. (2007). *The ISTE national educational technology standards (NETS) and performance indicators for students*. Eugene, OR: International Society for Technology in Education.

Jellison, J. A. (2000). How can all people continue to be involved in meaningful music participation? In Madsen, C. K. (Ed.). *Vision 2020: The housewright symposium on the future of music education*. Reston, VA: Music Educators National Conference.

Jensen, E. (1998). How julie's brain learns. *Educational Leadership 56*(3), 41–45.

Jensen, E. (2005). *Teaching with the brain in mind* (2nd ed.). Alexandria, VA: Association for Supervision and Curriculum Development.

Josephson Institute. (2008a). *Making ethical decisions: The six pillars of character*. Retrieved from charactercounts.org website: http://josephsoninstitute.org/MED/MED-2sixpillars.html

Josephson Institute. (2008b). *The ethics of American youth: 2008*. Retrieved from charactercounts.org website: http://charactercounts.org/programs/reportcard/2008/index.html

Juchniewicz, J. (2007). Band directors' preferences and attitudes on the implementation of non-traditional music classes (abstract). *2007 Research perspectives in music education*. Florida Music Educators' Association. Retrieved from http://www.flmusiced.org/rpmepurchase/content/Article1.aspx

Kalkavage, P. (2006). The neglected muse. *American Educator 30*(3). Retrieved from http://www.aft.org.pubs-reports/american_educator/issues/fall2006/muse.htm

Kendall, J. S. & Marzano, R. J. (2004). *Content knowledge: A compendium of standards and benchmarks for K-12 education*. Aurora, CO: Mid-continent Research for Education and Learning. Available at http://www.mcrel.org/standards-benchmarks/

Kick, F. (1992, Fall). Junior high/middle school leadership: Testing the waters in a raging sea of hormones. *Today's Music Educator*, 29.

Kizlik, B. (2009, January). How to write learning objectives that meet demanding behavioral criteria. Boca Raton, FL: Adprima. Retrieved from http://www.adprima.com/objectives.htm

221

Knight, A. B. (2006) *Teacher Credibility: A tool for diagnosing problems in teacher/student relationships*. Retrieved from University of Oklahoma Program for Instructional Innovation website: http://www.ou.edu/pii/tips/ideas/credibility.html

Kratus, J. (2007). Music education at the tipping point. *Music Educators Journal 94*(2), 42–48.

learn, def. 1 (2009). In *Merriam-Webster Online Dictionary*. Retrieved from http://www.merriam-webster.com/dictionary/learn

learning, def. 1. (2009). In *Merriam-Webster Online Dictionary*. Retrieved from http://www.merriam-webster.com/dictionary/learning

learning, def. 2. (2001). In *The New Oxford American Dictionary* (2nd ed.). Oxford University Press. Retrieved from Oxford American Dictionaries [computer software].

learning, def. 3. (2001). *WordNet* 1.7.1. Princeton University. Retrieved from Webster's Online Dictionary website: http://www.websters-online-dictionary.org/definition/learning

Listen Up. (n.d.). [Brochure]

macro-, def. 1. (2009). In *Encarta World English Dictionary* (North American edition). Retrieved from http://encarta.msn.com/dictionary_/macro-.html

Madsen, C. & Madsen, C. (1983). *Teaching discipline: A positive approach for educational development*. Raleigh, NC: Contemporary Publishing.

Mager, R. F. (1975). *Preparing instructional objectives* (2nd ed.). Belmont, CA: Fearon.

March, T. (2006). The new WWW: Whatever, whenever, wherever. *Educational Leadership, 63*(4), 14–19.

Marshall, M. (2001). Promoting learning: The power of positivity – Part 2. *teachers.net Gazette 2*(2). Retrieved from http://teachers.net/gazette/ FEB01/marshall.html

Marzano, R. J. (1992). *A different kind of classroom: Teaching with dimensions of learning.* Alexandria, VA: Association for Supervision and Curriculum Development.

Marzano, R. J. (2000). *A new era of school reform: Going where the research takes us.* Aurora, CO: Mid-continent Research for Education and Learning. Retrieved from http://www.mcrel.org/PDF/ SchoolImprovementReform/5002RR_NewEraSchoolReform.pdf

Marzano, R. J. (2007). *The art and science of teaching.* Alexandria, VA: Association for Supervision and Curriculum Development.

Marzano, R. J., Pickering, D. J., & McTighe, J. (1993). *Assessing student outcomes: Performance assessment using the dimensions of learning model.* Alexandria, VA: Association for Supervision and Curriculum Development.

Marzano, R. J., Pickering, D. J., & Pollock, J. E. (2001). *Classroom instruction that works: Research-based strategies for increasing student achievement.* Alexandria, VA: Association for Supervision and Curriculum Development.

Maxwell, J. C. (1991). *The 21 Irrefutable Laws of Leadership.* Nashville, TN: Thomas Nelson Publishers.

Maxwell, J. C. (1998). *The 21 irrefutable laws of leadership.* Nashville, TN: Thomas Nelson Publishers.

McEwan, E. (2001). *10 traits of highly effective teachers: How to hire, coach, and mentor successful teachers.* Thousand Oaks, CA: Corwin Press.

McTighe, J. & O'Connor, K. (2005, November). Seven practices for effective learning. *Educational leadership 63*(3). Alexandria, VA: Association for Supervision and Curriculum Development. 10–17.

McTighe, J. & Wiggins, G. (1999). *The understanding by design handbook.* Alexandria, VA: Association for Supervision and Curriculum Development.

Meier, D. (1995). The power of their ideas: Lessons for America from a small school in Harlem. Boston: Beacon Press.

MENC. (1994). The school music program: A new vision. The K-12 national standards, pre-K standards, and what they mean to music educators. Reston, VA: Music Educators National Conference.

MENC. (1997). *Where we stand*. Retrieved from https://www.menc.org/information/prek12/stand.html

MENC. (1999). *The value and quality of arts education*. Retrieved from http://www.menc.org/about/view/the-value-and-quality-of-arts-education

MENC. (2007, November 14). Midweek meanderings and miscellany XXXV: *Why? (this unfairness?!)...and Why? (we do it)*. Inside MENC (Blog). Retrieved January 9, 2009, from http://insidemenc.blogspot.com/2007/11/midweek-meanderings-and-miscellany-xxxv.html

MENC. (2008). [Banner on home page]. Retrieved January 20, 2009, from http://www.menc.org/

MENC Centennial Congress. (2007). MENC centennial declaration. *Teaching Music 15*(2), 11.

MENC Task Force on National Standards. (2007, October). *Report to the MENC national executive board*. Reston, VA: Music Educators National Conference. Retrieved from http://www.menc.org/publication/books/NEBreport10012007.html

Miceli, J. S. (2003, October). Making connections in music teacher education. *The School Music News*, 22–23.

Missouri Department of Elementary and Secondary Education. (1996). *The show-me standards: Overview of performance standards*. Retrieved from http://dese.mo.gov/standards/process.html

Missouri Department of Elementary and Secondary Education. (2007, May). *Missouri music grade-level expectations*. Retrieved from http://dese.mo.gov/divimprove/curriculum/GLE/music_gle_0607.pdf

musicianship, def. 1. (2009). In Cambridge Dictionaries Online. Retrieved from Cambridge Dictionaries Online: http://dictionary.cambridge.org/define.asp?key=52614&dict=CALD

223

National Education Association. (2003). *Status of the American public school teacher 2000-2001*. Washington DC: National Education Association.

Nitko, A. J. & Brookhart, S. M. (2006). *Educational assessment of students* (5th ed). Englewood Cliffs, NJ: Prentice Hall.

North Carolina Department of Public Instruction. (2000). *North Carolina arts education standard course of study: Music*. Retrieved from http://www.ncpublicschools.org/curriculum/artsed/scos/music/index

North Central Regional Educational Laboratory & Metiri Group. (2003). *enGauge 21st century skills: Literacy in the digital Age*. Retrieved from http://www.ncrel.org/engauge/skills/skills.htm

Northwest Regional Educational Laboratory. (2005). *Focus on effectiveness: Research-based strategies*. Retrieved from http://www.netc.org/focus/strategies/

objective, def. 1. (2001). In *The New Oxford American Dictionary* (2nd ed.). Oxford University Press. Retrieved from Oxford American Dictionaries [computer software].

Partnership for 21st Century Skills. (2007). *Framework for 21st century learning*. Retrieved from http://www.p21.org/documents/P21_Framework.pdf

Patterson, J. & Kim, P. (1991). *The day America told the truth*. New York: Prentice Hall.

Payne, R. K. (1996). *A framework for understanding poverty*. Highlands, TX: Aha! Process, Inc.

perfect, def. 1. (2001). In *The New Oxford American Dictionary* (2nd ed.). Oxford University Press. Retrieved from Oxford American Dictionaries [computer software].

Perfect, T. J. & Schwartz, B. L. (2002). *Applied metacognition*. Cambridge University Press.

Perkins, D. (1993). Teaching for understanding. *American Educator 17*(3), 28–35. Retrieved from http://www.exploratorium.edu/IFI/resources/workshops/teachingforunderstanding.html

Popham, W. J. & Baker, E. L. (1970). *Systematic instruction*. Englewood Cliffs, NJ: Prentice Hall.

Poplin, M. & Weeres, J. (1993). Listening at the learner's level. *The Executive Educator 15*(4), 14–19.

prepared, def. 1. (2009). In *Encarta World English Dictionary* (North American edition). Retrieved from http://encarta.msn.com/dictionary_/prepared.html

professional, def. 1. (2001). In *The New Oxford American Dictionary* (2nd ed.). Oxford University Press. Retrieved from Oxford American Dictionaries [computer software].

purposeful, def. 1. (2001). In *The New Oxford American Dictionary* (2nd ed.). Oxford University Press. Retrieved from Oxford American Dictionaries [computer software].

real, def. 1. (2009). In *Encarta World English Dictionary* (North American edition). Retrieved from http://encarta.msn.com/dictionary_/real.html

reflection, def. 1. (2009). In *Encarta World English Dictionary* (North American edition). Retrieved from http://encarta.msn.com/dictionary_/reflection.html

Reimer, B. (2004). Reconceiving the standards and the school music program. *Music Educators Journal 91*(1), 33–37.

Reimer, B. (2008, Spring). Achieving musical knowing. *Con Brio*. Chicago: DePaul School of Music.

Richards, H. V., Brown, A. F., & Forde, T. B. (2006). *Addressing diversity in schools: Culturally responsive pedagogy*. Tempe, AZ: National Center for Culturally Responsive Educational Systems.

Rosenshine, B. (1997). Advances in research on instruction. In J. W. Lloyd, E. J. Kameenui, & D. Chard (Eds.). *Issues in educating students with disabilities* (pp. 197–221). Mahwah, NJ: Lawrence Erlbaum Associates.

San Antonio, D. M. (2006). Broadening the world of early adolescents. *Educational Leadership 63*(7). Alexandria, VA: Association for Supervision and Curriculum Development. 8–13.

Sass, E. (1989). Motivation in the college classroom: What students tell us. *Teaching of Psychology 16*(2), 86–88.

Saunders, M. (2004, September). [Review of the book *Analyzing popular music*]. *Music Educators Journal, 91*(1), 64–65.

Schmoker, M. (1999). *Results: The key to continuous school improvement* (2nd ed.). Alexandria, VA: Association for Supervision and Curriculum Development.

Schmoker, M. (2001). *The results fieldbook: Practical strategies from dramatically improved schools.* Alexandria, VA: Association for Supervision and Curriculum Development.

self-aware, def. 1. (2001). In *The New Oxford American Dictionary* (2nd ed.). Oxford University Press. Retrieved from Oxford American Dictionaries [computer software].

Sheldon, K. M. & Biddle, B. J. (1998, Fall). Standards, accountability, and school reform: perils and pitfalls. *Teachers College Record (100)*1. 164–180.

-ship, def. 1. (2001). In *The New Oxford American Dictionary* (2nd ed.). Oxford University Press. Retrieved from Oxford American Dictionaries [computer software].

-ship, def. 2 (2009). In *Merriam-Webster Online Dictionary*. Retrieved from http://www.merriam-webster.com/dictionary/-ship

skill, def. 1. (2001). In *The New Oxford American Dictionary* (2nd ed.). Oxford University Press. Retrieved from Oxford American Dictionaries [computer software].

skill, def. 2. (2009). In *Encarta World English Dictionary* (North American edition). Retrieved from http://encarta.msn.com/dictionary_/skill.html

skill, def. 3 (2009). In *Merriam-Webster Online Dictionary*. Retrieved from http://www.merriam-webster.com/dictionary/skill

Steinberg, L. (1996). *Beyond the classroom.* New York: Simon and Schuster.

Stillings, N. A., Weisler, S.E., Chase, C.H., Feinstein, M.H., Garfield, J.L. & Rissland, E.L. (1995). *Cognitive science: An introduction* (2nd ed.). Cambridge, MA: The MIT Press.

Strong, J. H. (2002). *Qualities of effective teachers.* Alexandria, VA: Association for Supervision and Curriculum Development.

Strong, R., Silver, H. F., & Perini, M. (2001). Making students as important as standards. *Educational Leadership 59*(3), 56–61.

Strong, R., Silver, H. F., & Robinson, A. (1995). What do students want (and what really motivates them)? *Educational Leadership 53*(1), 8–12.

Suckling, J. (2005). Portraits of perfection. *Wine Spectator 30*(1), 56–66.

Sullivan, P. (2005, November 12). Management visionary Peter Drucker dies. *The Washington Post*, B06.

tenacious, def. 1 (2009). In *Merriam-Webster Online Dictionary*. Retrieved May 9, 2009, from http://www.merriam-webster.com/dictionary/tenacious

Thiagarajan, S. (2001, July). *Using thirty-five for debriefing. Play for performance* [e-newsletter]. Retrieved from http://www.thiagi.com/pfp/IE4H/july2001.html#DebriefingGame

Thompson, J. D. (2007). American idol and the music classroom: A means of critiquing music. *Music Educators Journal 91*(1), 36–40.

Tomlinson, C. A. (2002, September). Invitations to learn. *Educational Leadership 60*(1), 6–10.

U.S. Census Bureau. (March, 2005). Table 1a, Percent of high school and college graduates of the population 15 years and over, by age, sex, race, and hispanic origin: 2004. *Current Population Survey* [Data file]. Retrieved from http://www.census.gov/population/socdemo/education/cps2004/tab01a-01.pdf

Webb, L. (2000). The red shoe. *Educational Leadership 58*(1), 74–76.

West Virginia Department of Education. (n.d.). *Teach 21 instructional guides*. Retrieved from http://wvde.state.wv.us/instructionalguides/

Westwater, A. & Wolfe, P. (2000). The brain-compatible curriculum. *Educational Leadership 58*(3), 49–52.

Whitehead, A. N. (1929). The aims of education and other essays. New York: Free Press.

Wiggins, G. (1998). Educative assessment: Designing assessments to inform and improve student performance. San Francisco: Jossey-Bass.

Wiggins, G. (2007, November 15). *What is an essential question?* Retrieved from authenticeducation.org website: http://www.authenticeducation. org/bigideas/article.lasso?artId=53

Wiggins, G. (2008, December 9). *A conversation with Grant Wiggins: Habits of mind.* Retrieved from authenticeducation.org website: http://www. authenticeducation.org/bigideas/article.lasso?artId=48

Wiggins, G. & McTighe, J. (1998). *Understanding by design.* Alexandria, VA: Association for Supervision and Curriculum Development.

Wiggins, G. & McTighe, J. (2006). *Understanding by design* (2nd ed.). Upper Saddle River, NJ: Pearson.

Williams, L V. (1983). *Teaching for the two-sided mind.* Englewood Cliffs, NJ: Prentice-Hall.

Willingham, D. T. (2004). Students remember…what they think about. In *Annual editions: Educational psychology 04/05* (pp. 74-78). New York: McGraw-Hill.

Willingham, D. T. (2009). *Why don't students like school? A cognitive scientist answers questions about how the mind works and what it means for the classroom.* San Francisco, CA: Jossey-Bass.

Wisconsin Department of Public Instruction. (1997, June). *Wisconsin model academic standards for music.* Retrieved from http://dpi.wi.gov/ standards/pdf/music.pdf

Wiske, M. S. (Ed.). (1998). *Teaching for understanding: Linking research with practice.* San Francisco: Jossey-Bass.

Wolfe, P. & Brandt, R. (1998, November). What do we know from brain research? *Educational Leadership 56*(3), 8–13.

Woo, Y., Herrington, J., Agostinho, S., & Reeves, T. C. (2007). Implementing authentic tasks in web-based learning environments. *Educause Quarterly 30*(3). 36–43. Retrieved from http://net.educause.edu/ir/ library/pdf/EQM0735.pdf

www.SongLyrics.com. Accessed April 12, 2010.

Zeeman, E. C. (1977). *Catastrophe theory: Selected papers, 1972–77.* Reading, MA: Addison-Wesley.

a conversation with the author

What is the first thing you would say to a reader of this book?

After thank you(!), I would remind the reader that Destinations is only a spark. For every topic within, the underlying challenge is transfer—applying and adapting the ideas to unique contexts.

What is the overarching message in this book, the most important thing you hope readers will take with them?

A giant leap toward answering two monumental questions: "Under what conditions is learning most likely to occur?" and "How can I make the most of my reign in music education?"

Since the release of your first book, *Pathways*, what do know now that you didn't know then?

I know that persistence is highly underrated. You have to dig, investigate, and swirl things around in your mind before the complexities of effective teaching really begin to make sense. There is no fast track to wisdom. In time, through strategic action, reflection, revision, and an incessant quest to answer the questions that will inevitably arise, not only will student growth and achievement improve, but you will also be able to infer why it improved. This process will bring even more questions, which explains the never-ending climb of the committed educator.

I know that complacency—accepting the status quo of participation—is an eminent threat to music education. As a profession, we have to find a way to reach more students, to connect in meaningful ways with a much larger percentage of the student population. To do this, we have to connect "school music" with reality. Think about it. In what subject area other than music is there a clear distinction between what goes on in school and what goes on out of school? Fortunately, it is quite possible to preserve traditions while starting new traditions. Unfortunately, alteration is a foe. Everyone wants to get better; few want to change. Until more are uncomfortable with the theme, there will be little momentum for variation.

I know that far too many students want something for nothing, which of course is equivalent to cheating themselves. It's rare but wonderful when a student comes up and says, "I really want to learn more about this and I was hoping you could show me the way." After the shock and awe subsides, it's always a great experience. This is also a sign that the student is discovering one of the most important lessons of all—there is no finish line in learning.

I know that teaching is unrivaled in reward. Although some days you're the dog and some days you're the hydrant, teaching bestows us with the honor of shaping those who will shape tomorrow. This is something to take very seriously, but it's also very much a blessing.

If someone where to criticize this book, what would you say?

James McCosh (1811–1894), philosopher of the Scottish School of Common Sense and former President of Princeton University, says it far better than I can: "The book to read is not the one which thinks for you, but the one which makes you think."

Any final thoughts?

Yes. Anna Nalick recorded a song called "Breathe (2 AM)." There are lyrics in this song that perfectly capture my thoughts about this book:

2 AM AND I'M STILL AWAKE, WRITING A SONG

IF I GET IT ALL DOWN ON PAPER, IT'S NO LONGER INSIDE OF ME,

THREATENING THE LIFE IT BELONGS TO

AND I FEEL LIKE I'M NAKED IN FRONT OF THE CROWD

'CAUSE THESE WORDS ARE MY DIARY, SCREAMING OUT LOUD

AND I KNOW THAT YOU'LL USE THEM, HOWEVER YOU WANT TO

ANNA NALICK • "BREATHE (2AM)"

about the author

Joseph Alsobrook has been an active music educator since 1988. He currently serves as Chairman of the Music Department at Lindenwood University in St. Charles, Missouri. Prior to his current position, Mr. Alsobrook taught instrumental music at Union High School and Union Intermediate High School in Tulsa, Oklahoma. His fifteen years of classroom experience includes elementary music, middle school band, and high school band and orchestra. The positive impact Mr. Alsobrook has on student achievement is evident by his extensive list of noteworthy awards. This includes countless superior performance ratings, a concert performance at the Oklahoma Music Educators Association conference, and top honors at the Fiesta Bowl National Pageant of Bands, the Citrus Bowl Music Festival, the Tournament of Roses Parade, and multiple regional and national events sponsored by Bands of America.

Mr. Alsobrook has been a guest speaker on music education in several states, is certified in Early Adolescence through Young Adulthood Music by the National Board for Professional Teaching Standards, and is a six-time recipient of the Outstanding Achievement Music Director's Award presented by the Oklahoma Secondary Schools Activities Association. In 2005, he was recognized as a Distinguished Mentor by Lindenwood University and is the 2009–2010 Lindenwood University Scholar of the Year.

Mr. Alsobrook is author of *Pathways: A Guide for Energizing and Enriching Band, Orchestra, and Choral Programs* (2002) and *Destinations: A Compass for K–12 Music Educators* (2011). Both texts are published by GIA Publications, Inc.

about the editor

Michael D. Worthy began teaching in 1989 and is currently an Associate Professor of Music at the University of Mississippi in Oxford, where he teaches instrumental music education courses, research courses, and directs the Mississippians Jazz Ensemble. He also supervises student teachers and graduate research projects. Prior to his appointment at the University of Mississippi in 2002, Dr. Worthy taught at Castleton State College in Vermont, where he directed the wind ensemble and established the Lakes Region Youth Orchestra Wind Ensemble, comprised of excellent high school musicians from Vermont and upstate New York. Dr. Worthy has also held teaching and conducting positions in Oklahoma and Texas. He has been a guest conductor, clinician, and adjudicator in Oklahoma, Texas, Vermont, New Hampshire, New York, New Jersey, Mississippi and Tennessee.

Dr. Worthy is an active researcher and has published scholarly articles in the *Journal of Research in Music Education*, the *Bulletin of the Council for Research in Music Education,* and the *Journal of Music Teacher Education*. His research interests include rehearsal techniques, repertoire, and jazz education. He is a founder and editor of the *Southern Music Education Journal* and has presented his research at state, regional, and national conferences across the country. Dr. Worthy was recently commissioned by Oxford University Press to write on jazz education topics in the forthcoming second edition of the *New Grove Dictionary of American Music* and the *Oxford Handbook of Music Education*.